"This is everyth. [...]
Program (ATA[...] [...] you. Best 2 hour read to
prepare you for the next chapter of your life."

—*CW4 Eric Collier, USA Ret.*

"Having worked with thousands of veterans and seeing
many struggle, it is great to see Nic Transtrum offer a real
solution for veterans to win in life after the military."

—*Sudip Bose, MD, FACEP, FAAEM | Combat
Veteran | Founder- www.TheBattleContinues.org*

"I transitioned out of the military after I had returned
home from Iraq in 2006. For a long time I struggled to
find my new mission and why I was here. I looked around
and saw people who had concerned themselves with the
most trivial of issues and felt that I had just lost my higher
purpose. I wish I would have had this book 10 years ago.
Finding my next "high-value target" would have been a
much more effective process. And, using the nine
overlooked gifts every veteran possesses would have been
invaluable as I strove to find new meaning in civilian life."

—*Ryan Michler, Combat Veteran | Founder- Order of Man*

"This book will help veterans realize the potential they have as they make the transition from the military to the private sector."

—CW4 Mark Borden, USA Ret.

"Each man and woman who sign on the dotted line walk through a door that changes them forever. It can be a change for the good or not so good once they try to walk back. Nic walked through the fire of getting his life back. From these fires this book gives veterans the tools they need to walk back through that door themselves and enjoy a fulfilled life they so bravely served to defend."

—Terry Johnson, Founder/President- Show of Support

"Every transitioning veteran should read this book. I wish it had been available when I exited the military."

—MSgt. Vincent Vanata, USMC Ret.

ADAPT

AND

OVERCOME

VETERANS *NO B.S.* FIELD GUIDE TO
WINNING AFTER THE MILITARY

NIC TRANSTRUM

Published by Ultimate Veteran Media
Blackfoot, ID 83221

ISBN: 978-0-9996091-0-1
Printed in the United States of America

For information about purchasing this book in bulk, educational materials or speaking engagements contact us at www.NicTranstrum.com

This book is dedicated to

Every veteran, spouse, parent and patriot who ever fought the good fight of transition to life after the military

...So that we may all enjoy the freedoms that we fought for!

Contents

1

So, You're Getting out of the Military?

We sleep soundly in our beds because rough men stand ready in the night to visit violence on those who would do us harm.
—Winston Churchill

Dear Friend (Or, if you prefer, Soldier, Sailor, Marine, Airman, Grunt, POG, Jarhead, Leg, Chord Puller...however you like to identify yourself),

Thanks for your combat service and congratulations on your ETS (ending your time in service). You may be asking yourself a simple question—now what?

I know how you feel. It's a time of mixed emotions. As this chapter closes in your life, you have a lot to reflect on. In combat, you carried out extraordinary missions that most Americans will never be able to fully understand. You trained for years to develop specialized skills and then you successfully applied those strengths in the combat battlefield when it really counted. You accomplished incredibly difficult tasks under pressure while facing the toughest adversities. You were valued for your critical role as part of a team of brothers (and sisters) who counted on you. You wear the uniform and your patches with pride, as you should. Now it is time to enjoy the freedoms for which you fought.

As you walk away from the many perks of the military, there are also many things you will simply never miss. For example, you'll never miss 0500 formation for PT or uniform inspections. You will never miss death-by-PowerPoint briefings. You will never miss mass punishment doing push-ups and suffering for some other knucklehead's dumb decisions in your unit. And who in the world will ever miss applying for weekend passes just so you can go home for Thanksgiving? That is if you are not tagged for staff duty over the holiday…right?

However, while you are relieved to no longer

answer to Uncle Sam and look forward to total freedom, you probably have many unanswered questions. You are wondering...what will daily life be like? What will you do for work? How will you provide for your family? Should you use your G.I. Bill and go back to school? What is your new purpose? Surely there are many programs dedicated to helping you transition, right?

I know exactly what you are going through. I have walked in your shoes. I fought the good fight in combat too. I stepped up to the tough missions. I dodged bullets and RPGs, carried out my missions, and survived the hard landings. I survived months on end of high adrenaline missions with minimal sleep and mediocre food. I worked with the best team of guys in the world. We saved each other's backs multiple times. They respected me and I respected them. We were our own Band of Brothers.

Combat is where I discovered my Combat Bucket List. Occasionally I found myself in a situation. You know the type that I'm talking about—those times when the poop hits the fan and the situation is escalating and things get hairy really quick. I faced my share of these moments in which I wasn't sure if I was going to make it out alive. In those tense moments, I created my own bucket list of things that I swore to the heavens that I was going to do if I ever made it home. I committed that if I made it home I would love my wife more deeply. I would play with my kids more. I would quit worrying about all the petty things that just don't matter. I would be a better leader in my own life, in my own family, in my work and business, in my neighborhood and community. I swore I would use my skills to be a force for good. I swore I would live life and enjoy the freedoms for which we were fighting. I'm sure you can relate to similar situations.

I swore I would live life and enjoy the freedoms for which we were fighting.

Here is the truth about what I discovered in the transition after the military into civilian life. All I wanted to do was go live my Combat Bucket List. Unfortunately, I fell hard into what I call the Transition Trap. I lost my way and wasn't truly living life. The challenge turned out to be much bigger than I expected. It was like taking ten steps backward. I felt a bit like Tony Stewart leaving NASCAR and going to drive for Uber instead.

It wasn't so much of a struggle to find work itself. I had plenty of skills and contacts. The real struggle was to find work that was actually meaningful and challenging to me—and to find circles where I felt as valued as I was back at my unit. It was difficult to work with civilians who seem to operate by a different standard than the high level of discipline and execution that we had in the military.

My challenges weren't with employment alone. After a while it was hard to find any school, degree, hobbies or interests that really mattered and seemed significant. I tried every transition program out there, VA and otherwise, but wasn't finding what I needed to be fulfilled and enjoy life.

The solution finally hit me like a ton of bricks when I realized the military gave me (and you) some special gifts that cannot be found anywhere else. These gifts give us a huge advantage in the civilian world. This was the turning point once I started focusing on these gifts and fell back on my training. I just needed to identify my new HVT (High Value Target) to go after in life and apply my strengths to accomplish it like a new mission. Once I did, I broke out of the rat race, my life truly took off, and I've been on fire ever since.

Please don't struggle like I did. It took me six long, painstaking years of being lost and bouncing around to discover the way to break out. And if you are already stuck in the Transition Trap, there is finally an easier way to break out and step up to the life you deserve so you can get after your unfinished business on your Combat Bucket List. You have so much untapped potential that you probably don't even realize.

After the amazing accomplishments you had in the military and with the discipline you perfected, you should aim to *thrive* in civilian life. Not settle. Not struggle to fit in and survive. Your life should be a promotion—not a ten steps backward demotion. Your family needs you. The business world needs you. The civilian world needs you. You are a leader.

In the military you constantly adapted to new missions, changing environments, and moving targets by creating new tactics to overcome each obstacle. *Adapt and overcome* is not only a common term but a winning formula for success. Your next step after the military is no different. The goal after the military is to adapt to the next level and overcome the common challenges and transition traps so you can live the freedoms you fought for.

I did this and you can too. There is an easier way and I'm going to show you how in this book. I'm going to teach you what the nine gifts are that you mastered on the combat battlefield, then show you how to apply them in the civilian world or veteran battlefield. By the way, did I mention you can make a whole lot of money with your military skills as well?

Once you realize your gifts, I'll help you identify your new HVT that you are passionate about and show you how to apply the nine gifts to engage and take the targets in your new life.

I can't stress enough how imperative it is that you understand who you are and what your mission is as you go into the next phase of your life.

The cause of freedom isn't limited just to your military service. You have a new role as a veteran to continue freedom. The veteran's role in freedom is clearly defined with these three laws of the Ultimate Veteran:

3 Laws of the Ultimate Veteran

1. Live the freedoms you fought for.

2. Identify your next HVT in life.

3. Make an impact.

How do you become an Ultimate Veteran? Live these three laws.

The key is identifying your next HVT so that you can step up and make an impact in your own life and the world around you. I'm going to show you exactly how to do that in these pages.

Thank you for trusting me.

Your brother,

2

What Type of Veteran Are You?

You've been told that you're broken, that you're damaged goods and should be labeled victims. I don't buy it. The truth, instead, is that you are the only folks with the skills, determination, and values to ensure American dominance in this chaotic world.
—James "Mad Dog" Mattis,
U.S. Secretary of Defense

There are three types of veterans. Or to put it more accurately, there are three different places that vets tend to end up. This is not a criticism. It's fact.

Why do they end up here? Frankly it's not their fault. Unfortunately, they didn't have sufficient direction through transition—until now.

Like many, I was very successful in the military. I

had a clear mission, a resolute sense of purpose, and knew exactly what was expected of me each and every day. Unfortunately after transitioning, I really struggled. I had been counting down the days until I could return to my civilian life, but I hadn't expected how it would feel when the entire infrastructure supporting me during my service went away. I was truly sucking wind.

If there's so much help out there for veterans transitioning out of the military, then why did I struggle so much?

The good news is I eventually broke through…in a big way. I created a life that I don't need a vacation from. I find ways to create massive value in the civilian world. And I credit my success to the strengths I acquired in the military. I ultimately learned that I had strengths and discipline that were unique to my experiences serving my country. This book contains the steps I took to redefine my life. It is my honor to now share this new direction to help you.

At one point after I found my new life, I had to question…if there's so much help out there for veterans transitioning out of the military, then why did I struggle so much? And why do so many other vets struggle? Something must surely be missing. This realization caused me to look back at my journey through the Transition Trap and the steps I took to redefine my life—and how I found my new High Value Target (HVT) to go after. I figured out who I was and what I wanted and how to use my skills to get it.

The three types of veterans breakdown is not a criticism of our brothers and sisters who fall into the Transition Trap. The truth is, in my roller coaster journey I have been through all three levels. So, I know what it's like. The struggle is real and we should all continue to support and encourage them to heal and rise up. God bless them and all those who commit to serve them.

So, what are the three types of veterans?

The Demoted Veteran (Broken)

These are vets who get out of the military and seem to take ten steps backward right away. They don't know who they are or what they want. They don't value themselves or their capabilities. They are demoted in life, purpose and paycheck. They get lost very quickly. They fail to improvise, adapt and overcome to their new circumstances out of the military. If they do land a job, they settle for below average. They struggle to just fit in and survive. They are often mentally broken and dependent on others (whether it's the VA, spouse, caregivers, Social Security) for survival.

I want to note that there is a very big difference between being physically broken and mentally broken. None of this has to do with being physically broken. Those who are suffering from physical disabilities need help—and there is surely nothing shameful about seeking out help after undergoing some potentially traumatic circumstances. No question. They need and deserve every help they can get. But I have many friends without legs and arms who are mentally strong and find their HVTs and are very successful in life.

Demoted Veterans are mentally broken—much like a defeated zoo lion that has lost his heart. They look at the world with a blank, subdued stare. No drive or purpose. No hope. They often struggle with PTSD and, even worse, they accept it won't get better. They lose their sense of self-worth and fail to find a place or cause that fully uses their skills and abilities. They often develop a victim mentality and sense of entitlement, which weakens their own ability to achieve and be successful. They struggle to create value in the civilian world and feel like there is no place where they fit into society, like they don't matter. The worst-case scenarios even end up on park benches or commit suicide. It truly is the shame of our nation that so many of our finest veterans find themselves in such a destitute position to this day, even after years of public awareness and efforts to stop the veteran homelessness epidemic. I have personally known far too many good men that have ended their lives through suicide because they didn't think they mattered anymore.

The Average Veteran (Stuck)

The Average Veteran is stuck being just that—average. This type of veteran exits the military and settles into an average job and average lifestyle. Their high achievement in the military becomes a thing of the past and they have a hard time demonstrating to their civilian co-workers all the skills they used in combat and how they can be leveraged. They struggle with nine-to-five jobs where they are stuck putting round pegs in round holes. They are haunted knowing they are capable of so much more but don't know what or how to go about starting. They aren't passionate about their work or contribution. Over time, they simply go nuts because they aren't using their high achiever skills. They want to be in on the action and be part of something successful again, but they don't know what or how.

The Ultimate Veteran (Thriving)

Ultimate Veterans step up to the next level after the military. They get massive promotions in life, career, income and lifestyle. How do they do it? The answer is simple. They identify their next HVT to go after in the civilian world. They are fully aware of their skills to achieve big targets. They are leaders in their lives, their families, their circles and in their business. They use their skills to influence and lead civilians and help pull them up. Money flows to them because they know how to create value and make a positive impact in the civilian world. Most of all, they enjoy the freedoms for which they fought for—namely they enjoy every aspect of life, liberty and the pursuit of happiness.

That is the ultimate goal, after all…to enjoy life, liberty and the pursuit of happiness. Don't ever lose sight of that.

You have a choice. You are the one who gets to decide what type of veteran you'll be. What's it going to be?

This book will give you the steps that you need to avoid getting stuck in the transition trap and get where you want to go. And it gives stuck vets a path to get unstuck and rise to the next level.

3

Beware of the Transition Traps

Uncommon valor was a common virtue.
—Admiral Chester Nimitz

In the following chapters of this book, I will show you the nine gifts that the military gave you—gifts that are your key to pursuing your next HVT. But be cautious—if you don't use all of your gifts, you risk your gifts becoming traps when you transition to the civilian world. These are the traps that create broken Demoted Vets and stuck Average Vets when they exit the military.

These Transition Traps are wide open manholes just waiting for you to fall into. They are unique to veterans. As a high achiever in the military, you have developed a unique drive as well as personal needs that have to be filled. You're used to hitting targets over and over. You can't just stop. You need to keep doing it. It's like the gas that fuels the machine. You have to have it or you can't function. If you find yourself stuck, digressing, lost, unfulfilled, lacking or feeling like you don't matter anymore in the way that you did when you were in the military, I can guarantee you that it's because of one or more of these transition traps.

Challenge Trap - The military trained you to be an Ultra-High Achiever. You were constantly entrusted with extraordinary tasks and big missions. After the military, vets get stuck in the Challenge Trap when they aren't challenged enough or are operating at a level below what they know they are capable of. Most often this takes place because they don't realize the potential of their skills and strengths so they settle for a lower ability level. The solution is to define a HVT that fuels your passion, pushes your limits, and allows you to grow and expand. Take heart and trust that you are an Ultra-High Achiever. Completing service in the United States military is not for the weak or the faint of heart; you have already accomplished something extraordinary and you surely can do it again. It's simply in your bloodstream that you must be challenged. You know that you are capable of so much more. You will not be satisfied with mediocre nine-to-five jobs where you simply go through the paces and wait for your next vacation to roll around. You should lead the civilian world in high achievement.

Identity Trap - In the military, your identity was never in question. You knew exactly who you were, what you were there for, and where you belonged. You literally wore your experience on your sleeve and everyone could see at a glance who you were when you were in uniform. Your uniform alone commanded respect and sent a signal that you were part of something much larger than yourself. You knew exactly where you fit into the broader ecosystem. After the military, vets get stuck in the Identity Trap when they aren't sure who they are anymore or where they belong. They become lost and confused and they struggle to fit into the very different norms and rules of the civilian world ecosystem that doesn't know how to recognize or utilize their strengths and experience. They struggle to be valued like they were in the military. Once again, this happens when they don't realize their potential and they settle for less than they are capable of.

The solution is to become an Ultimate Veteran. You will excel in the civilian world when you are clear on who you are and what it is that you are about. You should lead the civilian world with your clarity and confidence in your identity. You know exactly who you are and what you are all about.

Objective Trap - The military gave you clear purpose. There was never a need to sit around reconsidering what the bigger picture was, because your mission was clear as day to you. You knew what you wanted and had a vision of where you were going. And the objective was tied to a deeply rooted cause—the cause of fighting for freedom, just as previous generations of Americans have done when they were summoned to battle in our moments of greatest conflict. After the military, these vets get stuck in the Objective Trap when they don't know what they want and they settle for mediocre objectives and less than they are capable of achieving. This happens when they don't have an exciting objective with a motivating cause they can get behind so they settle on poor objectives. The solution is to move on from the past, face the future, and discover the next HVT to go after in life. You were capable of making an impact in the military so now it's time to make an impact in the civilian world. You should lead the civilian world in setting clear objectives.

If you find yourself stuck... I can guarantee you that it's because of one or more of these transition traps.

Mission Planning Trap - In the military you knew how to create a plan to accomplish the mission. You could plan the steps as well as the skills and resources necessary to win. After the military, vets get stuck in the Mission Planning Trap when they just don't know how to reach certain objectives. They want to accomplish big things but they get the planning wrong or they give up altogether simply because they don't know the steps. For example, many vets think that to obtain upper management jobs or start their own business that they have to go back to school to earn graduate degrees and work their way up the ladder. The truth is that the steps that

most civilians follow are not always the best
suited for Ultra-High Achiever Vets. This is
truthfully one of the prime benefits of military
service—you gain extraordinary qualifications and
skills that civilians could never attain in a
conventional work attitude. The solution is to
identify an HVT that enables you use your Ultra-
High Achiever skills from the military to lead and
impact the civilian world. You will quickly find
high level jobs or run your own business. You
should lead the civilian world in effective mission
planning.

Capabilities Trap - The military trained you
with specialized skills and abilities to reach your
objectives. You were proficient and had routine
habits that ensured that the job was completed.
After the military, vets get stuck in the
Capabilities Trap when they don't use their skills
and abilities. Most often this happens because
they settle for a job or lifestyle that doesn't allow
them to fully use their skills. This syndrome leads
to a demotion across the board in every area of
life—in jobs, pay and lifestyle. The solution is to
have a HVT that allows you to thrive by using
your skills and excel at what you are good at. You
are capable of more than most civilian jobs will
give you credit for. You have an abundance of

real world application skills and the experience required to accomplish big objectives. You should lead the civilian world in capabilities.

Balance Trap - In the military, you were physically and mentally tough. Your environment kept you balanced and focused. After the military, vets get stuck in the Balance Trap when they become physically and mentally weak. Most often this is due to the change in environment that lacks structure and allows poor habits and laziness to develop. The solution is to implement a new framework into your personal life. Your environment is critical to helping you remain a well-oiled machine. You should lead the civilian world in physical and mental strength.

Accountability Trap - The military provided a very structured environment for personal growth and peak performance. You had constant feedback, coaching and accountability that forced you to grow and be your best. After the military, vets get stuck in the Accountability Trap when they fail to grow and under-perform. This happens when they don't have accountability coaches that force them to be their best. The solution is to surround yourself with friends, groups and coaches who will pull you up and hold you accountable to be your best. You should lead the civilian world in peak performance.

Execution Trap - The military trained you to take action and execute on fundamentals to ensure success. Skilled execution is about making success happen and getting the job done. After the military, vets get stuck in the Execution Trap when they fail to take action or fail to execute on fundamentals. Most often this is because they fail to step up to the next level, and don't have clear focus or lack discipline. The solution is to take massive action and use your skills to accomplish your next HVT. You should lead the civilian world in precision execution.

Resource Trap - The military trained you to be connected and engaged with the people and resources necessary to carry out your mission. You either did the job yourself or you found the right person who could get it done. After the military, vets get stuck in the Resource Trap when they aren't connected to the right people or resources. Most often this happens because they have limited civilian world resources and they give up. The solution is to find and connect with the best civilian world people and resources necessary to carry out your new HVT mission.

You were resourceful in the military and you need to be resourceful in the civilian world to be effective. You should lead the civilian world in resourcefulness.

I know that I have presented a lot of challenges and landmines to navigate. But I have good news for you. The cure for each of the transition traps is in your next HVT. Once you discover your next HVT, you will avoid or move on from stuck, has been, burned out, not valued anymore, struggling, chaos, lost & undefined, demotion in life, broke emotionally, PTSD, unbalanced and disconnected and into the next level.

That means growing, expanding, accelerating, valued, making an impact, accomplishing things that matter, thriving, structure, focused and on purpose, promoted and attracting wealth, mentally and physically strong and high performance, balanced life, relationships, health, contribution, and staying connected and engaged.

A Word about PTSD

What about those who struggle with symptoms of PTSD? We all do to some extent. There are many symptoms, from anxiety, depression, and sleep insomnia to regret and guilt. The struggle is real. It isn't always easy to find meaning for acts of war and some of the horrific things you may have seen in combat. All I can say is that you have incredible experience that few others can ever match. You have performed in truly life or death situations, in which a team may have likely been dependent on your judgment and skills in order to come home safely. And if you can work your way through it and turn your focus from your own challenges to others, you can do a world of good by using your wisdom to help those around you. You have a lot to offer. Leaders at top levels draw deeply from their experience and wisdom to help pull people up—including painful experiences they may have gone through. You have a choice to bottle it all up or dig deep and learn from it so you can use that experience to help others. Great leaders know what their people are going through. It's called empathy. I'm sure George Washington had a lot of empathy when he took office as the first President of the United States.

I'm going to lay out a pretty bold claim for you— for many, HVT could be the solution for PTSD after the military. Now don't get me wrong; I'm not a doctor, counselor or psychiatrist. I can't legally make medical claims or give medical advice. But one thing I know for sure is that I never sat across the room from a shrink or VA doctor who had actually been in combat and felt and understood the struggles I was going through. There seemed to be zero empathy. They gave me the standard treatments that they learned to give—though they don't actually work.

Many will argue my claim here. They'll say I'm not qualified to make such a claim. They'll say studies have proven that their medicines and therapy treatments help. Sure, it certainly works for some. And I'm truly happy for those who it works for. And sure, the symptoms are better when you are drugged up. Insomnia is cured when you take enough sleep meds and you sleep all night and all day. Anxiety attacks are fewer, but you also can't feel anything when you talk to someone. Depression lows are not as bad when you're numb but you also don't have fun highs or enjoy life. In my experience, I have seen that these treatments help the symptoms but not the real problems. I have to ask the question—why are there so many veterans out there who seem to keep struggling?

So, what's the real problem? Ultra-High Achievers that become stuck. I suggest to you that PTSD symptoms are also the symptoms of Ultra-High Achiever men and women who have become caged lions. High achievers who once were so capable of extraordinary levels of operation and accomplishment are now restrained in new confines and limits of improperly defined arenas of operation. It's like a young champion race horse who is retired too early into a stable, never to race again. Ultra-High Achievers are no different. With such incredible abilities ready to be used, but bottled up and going to waste, it's no wonder they end up with symptoms of depression, anxiety, and insomnia. With the young race horse in mind, does it make sense that doctors and medications are the correct solution? Absolutely not. What makes sense is to saddle up that race horse and point it to a new track where it can keep winning races. The solution is a clearly defined HVT to pursue after the military.

Once I discovered my HVT, my life turned around dramatically. I had real purpose once again. I filled in the missing gaps. I was using my skills again. I was making an impact again.

This book is not focused on PTSD or treating

PTSD symptoms. It will, however, give you the framework to move on with an exciting life by finding new HVTs. As I realize many people reading this will be in the transition traps and struggling with PTSD, I created a bonus training to show you how I kicked PTSD in the teeth. You can access it here: www.NicTranstum.com/bookbonus.

Whatever you focus on grows. It is impossible to get rid of pesky PTSD if you stay in a world focused on it. HVT gives you a new world to focus on—and finally leave PTSD in the past.

Now let's dive into each of the nine gifts together.

4

Ultra-High Achiever: You Are a Rare Breed

I am a soldier. I fight where I am told,
and I win where I fight.
—General George Patton, Jr.

I went to visit with Bob in his gun store. Not only does Bob own the local gun store, but he is also the Command Sergeant Major of the local National Guard unit. I was in search of a story for my book—and I had a hunch that he would have something to share with me.

I was looking for a story illustrating the rare breed of ultra-high achievers in the military. We started to chitchat and before I could even tell him what I was looking for, his phone rang. I watched as he got a call about a possible upcoming deployment.

He was asked the question—if this activation happens, would he be willing to go?

He didn't even hesitate. Not for a second. Bob replied, "Hell yeah, I'd go back to Iraq in a heartbeat!"

I knew I had my story. I watched it unfold right in front of me.

Bob just proved my point. He is a busy man with a full life. Even though he has a business to run, a family at home, and a leadership role in the military, Bob didn't hesitate to step up to a tough challenge like going to combat again.

That's because Bob is part of a rare breed. He is an Ultra-High Achiever. He has years of experience of stepping up to the next level and conquering objective after objective. It is certainly no accident that he owns his own business and is a Command Sergeant Major. This is a mindset and a way of doing things.

I mentioned to him, "At one point you were offered a promotion to Staff Sergeant, and then to First Sergeant and on and on up the ladder. You knew it was going to be a lot more work and a lot more responsibility. Why did you take it?"

To which he replied, "Because it was an opportunity to step up. I was always working on improving myself and looking for new opportunities. Each new promotion comes with a new set of challenges. But I'm always up for a new challenge."

You are a rare breed. You are a real warrior. You have already proved yourself in combat—an experience unlike anything in civilian life.

Combat missions are remarkable experiences. They are among the highest form of achievement for a human being. It is simply amazing to be able to go anywhere in the world and work under incredibly adverse situations. You have the ability to change environments in an instant. You can apply your full range of skills and abilities, function physically, and focus mentally—all while creating a mission plan to accomplish a particular objective and then to take action, adapt and overcome, and ultimately take the target.

HVTs are not easily taken. Not just any Joe off the street can accept a mission to go into combat and successfully overtake a HVT. It requires a whole lot more than just willpower and courage.

It requires specialized mindset, specialized skills, training, conditioning, strategic planning, and precision execution. It requires a person with unwavering commitment and discipline to not quit when times get tough and bullets start flying. It requires someone special who is willing to sacrifice whatever it takes to get the job done. It requires an Ultra High Achiever.

Ultra-High Achievers are an ultra-rare breed. Ultra-High Achievers have to be challenged. After shooting 1,000 yards, they can just never be satisfied with 100-yard targets again. After a PT score of 300, they'll never be satisfied with a score of 250. They like to push the limits. They get used to achieving big things on a regular basis. Winning becomes addictive. Getting the job done becomes a daily standard.

You are an Ultra-High Achiever. You are wired for high achievement and you will simply not be satisfied in life until you fill the gaps in the civilian world. It's a bit like having an itch that needs to be scratched. Nothing else short of truly AWESOME achievements will make you happy, fulfilled or satisfied. Everything else will seem like it doesn't matter... because to you, it simply doesn't.

The military breeds Ultra-High Achievers and teaches them the skills they need to succeed at taking the biggest targets in the world. I'm not talking about your MOS-related skills like shooting, clearing a room, or performing first responder medical aid. I'm talking about all of your hidden skills that help you be an Ultra-High Achiever in the first place—traits such as leadership, communication, planning, execution, discipline, and more. I'm talking about the skills you have that allow you to go out and accomplish big things. I'm talking about the skills necessary to get the job done. They might be intangible or not easy to represent on a resume or LinkedIn profile, but you know that you can call upon them when the bad stuff hits the fan and times get really tough.

The military has given you a gift of being an Ultra-High Achiever. They helped you master the art of achievement and helped you master the skills necessary to accomplish big missions. They gave you just about the biggest playground in the world to learn, practice, hone and master your Ultra-High Achiever skills. You already have these skills. They are *super valuable*. Don't ever take them for granted. They cannot be taught in a classroom or a training program. They can only be learned through experience. I have to laugh when I sometimes hear various educational or training programs referred to as "boot camps" or civilians using war metaphors to describe their business dealings. I understand the image that they are trying to evoke, but it's laughable how wide a canyon there is between these fairly routine experiences and the true military experience. This reservoir of experiences and skills is your key to skipping to the front of the success line in the civilian world.

Watch out for the Challenge Trap; the military trained you to be an Ultra-High Achiever. You were constantly challenged with extraordinary tasks and big missions. After the military, vets often get stuck in the Challenge Trap when they aren't challenged enough by their new responsibilities. Most often this happens when they don't realize their potential and they settle for less than they are capable of achieving. The solution is to define a HVT that fuels your passion, pushes your limits, and allows you to grow and expand. You are an Ultra-High Achiever. You must be challenged. You know you are capable of more. You will not be satisfied with mediocre nine-to-five jobs putting round pegs in round holes. You should lead the civilian world in high achievement.

You were successful in combat with your Ultra-High Achiever skills. The civilian world and veteran battlefield are no different when it comes to success. At the end of the day, what matters is getting the job done (aka mission accomplishment). What matters is getting results. It's what makes the world go around, period. You just have to know what you want, create a plan to get it, and then execute.

You might think of your new life as an opportunity to take things easy. While you are certainly entitled to some of the rest and relaxation that you have rightfully earned, I submit to you that you will ultimately be much happier and more fulfilled if you continue to operate in high gear. You should achieve *more* by using your skills after the military...*not less*! Your life after the military should be a promotion, not demotion. You should be using your skills to be successful. You should be thriving and loving what you do and not struggling to fit in and survive and definitely not settling for LVTs (low value targets). You should accomplish more, influence more, lead better, and organize better. You should not sit by while guys who don't have a fraction of the skills and experience that you do run the civilian world around you. Your health, your bank account, your relationships should all be growing instead of getting lazy, fat and living paycheck to paycheck. After all that you have done and achieved while serving in the military, you should step up in life.

Don't underestimate your ability to truly thrive in the civilian world. Your biggest challenge is probably going to be realizing how much more you really are capable of and seeing what's possible for yourself. You have to be truly challenged or you'll go nuts. LVTs won't cut it. You need to fully understand what you are capable of. You need to understand what's possible.

Pick a HVT in your life that will challenge you and allow you to thrive by utilizing your Ultra-High Achiever skills.

You are a high achiever. You are different. You are capable of more. You are expected to be, know and do more.

Because you are a rare breed, you may have a difficult time finding a place in the civilian world. Here's why.

The civilian world that we all grew up in has a certain way of doing things. The people who inhabit this world all tend to have a certain way of seeing things. They have a certain perspective. Everything is laid out before them like a neat roadmap. For example, we grew up in public schools. After fifth grade comes sixth grade. After tenth grade is eleventh grade. After high school is college. And so on. It makes it very predictable and routine to expect what comes next. Why? So you can get a good education and then get a good job, like society expects.

The mindset doesn't end there. Life's milestones—job, house, family, comfortable retirement—are neatly rolled out with no need to think outside the box as long as you go along and don't rock the boat too much. I would estimate that this way of thinking makes up about 86 percent of America. I call this the low value target (LVT) civilian world job market. The LVT job market is a long-term, slow-paced retirement plan, clocking in at a nine-to-five job, putting round pegs in round holes 50 weeks a year in a job you don't love, and you get two weeks off for a vacation away from it all. All for what? A paycheck.

There's nothing necessarily wrong with this mindset. It allows for a comfortable, predictable routine that seems to work for many people. At least, it works in the sense of giving them a comfortable, relatively conflict-free daily life. They don't even need to spend much time thinking about how much more they are capable of. My primary critique of this mindset is that it doesn't allow for greatness—it encourages you to settle for so much less than you are truly capable of doing.

Then there's the military. They have a whole different mindset altogether. They have a different way of doing things. When you left the civilian world and joined the military, you had to change this way of thinking. Starting with boot camp, the military ecosystem breaks you down and builds you back up the way they need you to be. They essentially turn you into a completely different person—one that may still have the same talents and interests, but who brings much more discipline and rigor to how these gifts are used. Although it is a very structured environment, the military is in great need of people with special achievement skills to go around the world into adverse circumstances and perform extraordinary tasks under pressure to accomplish major objectives. They need Ultra-High Achievers. Only a rare breed of people are actually capable of doing this. You are part of this rare breed. You separated yourself from the civilian world the day you stepped up and joined the 0.5 percent that join military.

So where else do we see this pattern where high achievers separate themselves?

- Only 1 percent of Boy Scouts will achieve the highest rank of Eagle Scout.
- Only 1.6 percent of college football players will make it to the NFL.
- Only 5 percent of Americans make over $100K per year.
- Only 1 percent of Americans make more than $1 million per year.
- Only 14 percent of Americans own all the businesses, including the mom and pop shops that line main streets of small towns across rural America.

Do you see the pattern here?

These high achievers are not pushed into going above and beyond what is expected of them. They are self-driven; nobody does it for them.

They have to self-regulate and manage their own accomplishment.

When you see somebody thriving at the top of their game and firing on all cylinders, it is natural to ask what their secret to success is. What is it that sets them apart from the crowd?

The answer is that they fully commit to their mission. They don't just talk a big game about doing big things—the world is full of big talkers, hollow words, and empty promises. These folks actually follow through on their words and do the work. They finish the mission.

None of this has anything at all to do with luck. I am of the mind that you have to make your own luck and identify your own chances in this life. These people are also Ultra-High Achievers who eagerly step up to big challenges and go after big objectives. Part of it has to do with their innate character. They have the right mindset and the skills to back it up.

So where do you go after the military?

All of the transition programs will try to send you back to the LVT civilian world job market. They'll tell you to spice up your resume and find a job similar to your MOS. Or if you want to snag a "real job," you can go back to school and start all over again.

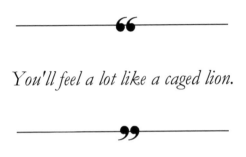

You'll feel a lot like a caged lion.

This didn't work for me. I tried it. And it very likely won't work for you either. You'll feel a lot like a caged lion. Why? Because you're an ultra-high achiever and you won't be satisfied in the LVT civilian world job market. They'll gladly hire you but they won't value the skills you have. They hire the 86 percent who march to a certain drum. They don't know what to do with Ultra-High Achievers. You'll be overqualified and underpaid. You'll have a hard time fitting in.

My friend Mike runs a thriving professional practice. Unfortunately, I have watched three different former military guys struggle to transition into this civilian business as partners. Each of them should have been a slam dunk. They had years of experience in the military, were good with their technical skills, and were very eager to join as a partner in Mike's business. But there's a different style in the civilian world and when it came to other interpersonal skills like how to treat clients or how to manage employees, they all fell way short. Mike vented his frustrations to me. "I thought they would be good partners because they are military, but they just simply don't understand how a business runs and they fail to adapt."

He was on his third candidate for the practice with a military background. It was not long before an argument broke out between the veteran and one of Mike's staff members. Frustrated and red in the face with anger, the veteran finally called out, "Don't you know who I was in the military? When I was in the military I never had to do that. I had 80 people under me who did all of that grunt work."

With some frustration apparent in his voice, his colleague replied, "Well that's not how it works around here." In the business world, we have to earn our customers and pay our own bills. It can be humbling to start over from a new position.

There is quite a gap. This vet is skilled and has a lot of invaluable experience to draw upon. He has

90 percent of the skills necessary to be effective in the civilian business, but he is failing to understand and adapt to the gap in his new environment. This scenario is far too common—I have seen it firsthand over and over again. Worse yet, it prevents good veterans from accessing good opportunities and pushes them into being average veterans.

A proper transition to the civilian world is badly needed. He needs to understand the gap and adapt to it to be 100% in the civilian game. But his real opportunity is when he closes that gap AND brings to the table all of his skills from the military that most civilians never learn so he can actually improve the business and add value in many ways. Believe it or not, closing the gap is actually a pretty simple fix.

It all comes back to the nine gifts—they truly are your key to HVT's in the civilian world. They are the same fundamentals used by top executives and business owners who count themselves among the top one percent of earners. These skills are not taught in school or any formal training programs. There is no degree or certification for them. They are the rare set of finely tuned and refined skills necessary to accomplish extraordinary tasks. You are in the top one percent with the same capabilities. You have just been on a different journey. Frankly you have undergone a more complex and higher stakes journey than most business professionals have ever gone through. After the HVTs that you pursued while in combat, you can now apply the same gifts to HVTs in the civilian world. It is the upper level equivalent of street smarts and real-world application of high achievement. The reputable and dependable people and units that always get tasked the import missions are the ones that encapsulate all nine gifts.

The only solution is to identify your next HVT to go after in the civilian world. This is your next big challenge to step up to, that you go to bed thinking about each night. Your next HVT might be an exciting business, a meaningful organization, or an upper management or executive job that suits you. This success world is chock-full of high achievers and you will find yourself fitting in much better. For example, only 14 percent of Americans have what it takes to be business owners. Many of these entrepreneurs are not even especially skilled or successful—they may lack formal business training and have never bothered to do the right kinds of market analysis to succeed long-term. But my hat still goes off to them, because they are the ones who step up to the challenge. They are the ones who are actively "in the arena," to borrow a famous term from Theodore Roosevelt. They are the ones who make the rules that run the LVT market.

There is no reason that you can't be doing the very same thing. Your skills are very similar to the successful high achievers in this world and you can achieve similar success. You possess the upper level equivalent of street smarts and real-world application of achievement. You know how to set big targets and how to accomplish them.

You are primed and ready. You just need your next HVT to go after.

Whatever you choose, I am confident that you will make an impact, step up and take your rightful place in the civilian world—then lead as you pull up other civilians around you.

The key is to remember that you must be challenged to be happy. I think this is something that a lot of us miss when we think of our notions of happiness. We may imagine being idle and relaxed. But there's a reason why so many older people begin to have health problems when they retire completely and disengage from their vocation—as people, we are hardwired to use our skills and pursue challenges.

I'll show you later how stepping up and being challenged ties into your HVT.

5

Identity: Who Are You?

What would you risk dying for—and for whom—is perhaps the most profound question a person can ask themselves. The vast majority of people in modern society are able to pass their whole lives without ever having to answer that question, which is both an enormous blessing and a significant loss.
—*Sebastian Junger*

It was mere days before he was to be deployed to Iraq. Sergeant Sam Deeds was notified that his Platoon Commander was not deploying with them. They needed a shift in leadership and so, the musical chairs began. When the music stopped, the former Platoon Sergeant stepped up to acting commander and Sam was thrown into the role as acting Platoon Sergeant. Even though Sam had just recently transferred to his unit from a recruiting job and lacked formal training as

Platoon Sergeant, he now faced the responsibility of leading 36 Marine Infantrymen into combat. The consequences of his decisions could have life or death implications for all of those around him.

Despite the fact that Sam was unsure of some of the details of being a Platoon Sergeant, he was able to rise to the challenge. He started by simply following core values and principles that are informally taught from day one of boot camp. He relied on fundamentals that are often quoted in the unit—adages *like know yourself and seek self-improvement, develop a sense of responsibility, restore hope and move on with a purpose, never leave a Marine behind, set the example for yourself,* and so on.

Sam brought one of the most invaluable traits available to his leadership style—humility. He acknowledged what he didn't know, even while stressing that his identity helped to guide his path. "I didn't know exactly what to do…but I knew I was a Marine Infantryman," he said. "I knew who I was and what I was there to do."

Sam knew that he could rely upon his *identity* for guiding his platoon. As a Marine Corps Infantryman, he knew exactly what his job was. He knew the mission. And when he went up and down his platoon of guys, in the simplest form of leadership, all he had to do was remind them who they were and they knew exactly what to do. It was a true model of inspirational leadership in action.

He didn't needlessly complicate things. He stuck to the basics like *every marine is a rifleman and a trigger puller first.* They knew what to do because they knew who they were.

"I went from being an infantryman to helping 36 infantrymen," he said. "We just knew we were infantrymen."

He supported his guys progressing from the A-Gunner moving up to 249 Saw Gunner. He intuitively knew what they needed. He had 36 guys to manage but in the end, it worked because they all knew who they were.

The day you joined the military you selected a MOS but little did you know you were selecting something much more than a job. You were also choosing an identity. Knowing *who* you were is another gift the military gave you. This gift has served you well, especially in the combat battlefield. When charging into battle, you knew exactly *who* you were. You had no doubt that your identity was an American War Fighter. With the clarity that comes along with knowing your exact place in the world, you also knew exactly what you had to do…fight the war and defeat the enemy. That is about as clear-cut as it gets. There was no confusion about the goal. You had total clarity regarding *who* you were when you stepped off that plane and your boots hit the sand. It was *go time.*

But be careful…you can easily miss that sense of clarity when it's gone.

Red alert! Watch out for the Identity Transition Trap. As long as you were in the military you knew exactly WHO you were and what you were about. But all that is about to change. Who exactly are you going to be after the military? When leaving the military, your job changes—but what about your identity? What happens to it?

Your identity is how you see yourself. It's what you stand for. It's where you belong, where you call home. It shapes who your brothers (and sisters) are. It determines who you associate with and drink beers with.

Your identity is reflected simply in the way you

show up and take care of business. Let's say for example that you enlisted into the infantry. You weren't any old grunt—oh no, you aspired for much more than that for sure. You wanted a Ranger tab. Not just because it was a cool patch, but because it would send a signal to those around you about your level of commitment.

It tells everyone who you are. After all, you didn't just buy the patch in a store—you earned it. You were specially selected from amongst your peers because of your high performance and readiness to grow.

You attended specialized training where you endured the beat-down rigors and pushed through your limits into new levels of skill and performance. Then you wore your Ranger tab with pride, signaling to every other soldier you walked past on base that you had achieved a higher level, that you stood out among your peers. You had earned the right of passage for yourself. You had joined the upper echelon of the Door-Kickers and you were proud to be a full-fledged, card-carrying member of the bad ass club.

Whether you were in the infantry or not, you get the point. It's a bit like the saying "you can learn a lot about a man by the shoes he is wearing." Well, you can learn a lot about a soldier literally by the patches that he wears. You see them everywhere. A right shoulder combat patch signals to everyone what unit you fought in combat with. They all say something very specific about the person wearing them. EIB (Expert Infantry Badge) sets you apart from standard infantry. EOD likes to blow stuff up. You know all the cues that tell you all you need. The green beret. The tan beret. The rank. The unit. Combat Action Badge. Aviator wings. Air Assault wings. Jump wings. Master Jump wings with a mustard stain.

News flash! You're not a soldier anymore.

You can also learn a lot about a person by the role they are in like the commander, the first sergeant, the platoon or team leader. It's *who* you are. It's your unique identity.

News flash! You are not a soldier anymore. The

environment that the military gave you to nurture your identity disappears forever when you get out, as difficult as that can be to accept at first. As much as it is a core part of your identity, the military will become a part of your past. Wearing the uniform will be part of your past. This is your wake-up call.

There are certain elements of your identity that will never die. I get it. "Once a Marine, always a Marine." Sure, that will never go away no matter what. For the rest of your life, you will wear the proud mantle of veteran. You may even ultimately choose to have your status as a veteran reflected in your final resting place when you pass from this life. But as essential as this identity is to your conception of yourself, you also need to be facing toward the future. You will find yourself in a very awkward situation if years from now you are still walking around town in your uniform telling people you're still a Marine.

People never ask *who are you*, but instead they learn who you are by asking *what you do*. Think about it. When you meet somebody one of the first things they ask you is, "What do you do?" This might not be as common in other parts of the world, but Americans place a huge part of our identity in what we do for a living. That's simply one of the most common ways we learn about somebody when we meet them. Although it's generalizing, we tend to get a quick picture about somebody as soon as they tell us they are an electrician, an engineer, a teacher, a business owner or retired. It allows us to get a sense of how they spend their days and where their talents lie.

Don't try to just blend in with the crowd. It might be tempting given how the military encourages you to think of yourself as part of a bigger unit than yourself—one in which your individual ambitions are secondary to supporting your team.

While teamwork is an integral part of success, achievement in the civilian world is much more oriented toward individual achievement. You are capable of much, much more. After all the skills you developed in the military, you can step up in the civilian world and promote yourself to the next level. You have the capabilities to accomplish anything you set your mind to after the military. But you will go nowhere as long as you lack a core identity. You will bounce around like a pinball and you'll struggle to fit in and survive. It is critical that you decide the next steps for your identity. In order to go after your new HVT (High Value Target) in your life, you have to be clear how your identity and how your past military skills evolve. When you are clear about who you are and what you want, then you are truly unstoppable.

Remember—your identity is how you see yourself. It's what you stand for. It's where you belong, where you call home. It shapes who your brothers (and sisters) are. It determines who you associate with and drink beers with—and how you show up and take care of business.

The military helps you know your identity. Your identity starts by saying, "I am _____."

Like any culture, you pick up your own language and terminology. Do any of these sound familiar?

The Few. The Proud. The Marines!

I am a "Marine."

I am an "Army of One."

All of these sayings trigger vivid feelings in me, wherever I hear them. They are all deeply intertwined with my sense of identity. Your main identity had sub-identities attached to it. The First

Sergeant might have been your identity, or it might have been as a commander.

The Unit you were in was also an identity in itself. No matter where you go in life, you will also answer to the name your group gave itself.

Phoenix. Rakkasans. Phantoms. Lancers. Balls. EZ Company.

For you, a "grunt" isn't a sound—it's an identity. And your identity has different labels attached to it. When charging into battle, you knew exactly who you were, why you were there, and what you were going to do.

Identity is who you are, and who you are not. "I'm not a soldier, I'm a Marine." I'm not a ____, I'm an Eleven-Bravo." I'm not a Sir, I work for a living." Do any of these sound familiar to you?

I was a Blackhawk Pilot, specifically trained for Air Assaults. It was a different mindset. It was an attitude. It was a focus.

I had friends that were Medivac pilots. They had a slightly different mindset about their missions. The Apache Pilots are all about guns. The Chinook Pilots are all about big engine power and picking up heavy lift loads.

But regardless of what it was in your specific instance, the military gave you a gift of Identity.

I always knew exactly who I was and what I was about. It might have felt stifling at times to you, but it's also a luxury that few will know in a society where so many are clearly searching for some type of purpose.

In contrast, I didn't have to worry about that. I knew who I wasn't and what I wasn't about.

I knew my role and how it fit in with other roles in a team.

For several years after I got out of the military, people would ask…"What do you do?" I would so often fall back on referring to the past. "I used to be in the military."

It could be hard for them to relate to that strong sense of identity I had that was so tied up in my past. While your military career was largely tied to your identity, it isn't necessarily so in the civilian world. Many people simply hate their jobs. They don't like being there. They aren't comfortable. They can't wait for the day to be over and the weekend can't come quickly enough.

So why do they stay?

It's simple. They settle. They need the money and they don't care to do what's necessary to make a change.

Why put yourself through that? You have doubtlessly tackled bigger challenges than fear of losing a job or enduring a temporary dip in income. After the prospect of deployment to Iraq or Afghanistan, there isn't a whole lot to be scared about out there.

Just the same, many people are lost and don't know who they are or what their identity is.

They are reacting to their circumstances. They desperately need money so they settle for a job they hate. Don't make that mistake. The solution is to align your identity with your career, job, business or however you choose to contribute.

My observation from seeing all the different ways that my fellow service members react to this transition is that identity gives you a sense of security. You will know if you start lacking in identity when you feel lost. As you look at the civilian world, you will start to explore next steps. Job. College. Retirement. But who are you now?

I was stuck in the Identity Transition Trap and it took me years to figure out how critical identity is during transition. Every time I met somebody new in the civilian world, I introduced myself and they usually asked, "What do you do?"

To which I replied, "Well…I used to be in the military, and now I do web design." Or sometimes I'd say, "I used to be a Blackhawk pilot, but now I do home inspections." Somehow the answer was always "I used to be" followed by whatever I was doing at the time. I wasn't even aware I was saying it. One day I realized it was impossible for me to introduce myself without prefacing *what I do* with my military past. It was such a critical part of my identity I had to tell them. After all, I'm not just any old website designer or home inspector. I couldn't possibly let people start to size me up without them knowing this significant tidbit of info about me, right?

Watch out for the Identity Transition Trap. You may feel lost, confused, trying to be somebody you're not. You don't know who you are now. Some other signs that you may notice:

1.   Lacking identity, don't know who you are or what you want

2.   Trying to be who you need to be to fit in

3.   Not trying to step up, move on, redefine the next phase, fail to move forward

4.   Feeling like you don't matter like you used to

Being a Veteran is an identity. It's different than active duty military—it's something that never goes away for life. For many, this transition away from it being an active part of daily life can be awkward for many years. Many don't know whether to claim their military service or not. They may find themselves confronted with the identity question when they least suspect it—like at the movie theater when confronted with a Veteran discount. "Am I a Vet or not?"

Average Vets have an awkward time at work trying to explain the incredible accomplishments they had in the military while also trying to explain why they are in an average nine-to-five job.

It can be difficult to transition identity. Most civilians appreciate veterans. But…not when it comes to employment. You might be very be very surprised how many job interviews occur where people will essentially say something to the effect of "Cool, thanks for your service, but where's your degree? How many years have you spent in civilian jobs? Have you checked all the right boxes?" After putting your life on the line defending freedom, it can be more than a little frustrating to learn that your prospects are entirely all about civilian rank and civilian time in service.

Sometimes you'll be proud of your service and veterans. Fly your flags, wear the shirts and hats. You will ride for the brand.

But not every day. It can be exhausting to always be donning the uniform and the mantle of the service. There are plenty of other times when you will find yourself to be ashamed of Demoted Vets—the ones who are broke, sleeping in the streets, struggling to fit in and even survive. Sure, they need help. But how is it that this rare breed who were once so capable of accomplishing major objectives have become so lost that they can't even provide for themselves? They have given up their independence when they are dependent on others for basic needs and survival. And what is the image they are projecting for veterans? As a result we have thousands of organizations dedicated to freebies and handouts for the vets. Other Demoted Vets are frustrated because they don't know who they are, but they don't want help, pity and handouts, so they're just mad at the world. Demoted Vets often feed on pity and sympathy.

Let's talk about disabled veterans for a moment. Disabled Vet is an identity that many build a lifestyle around. I want to clear this up right up front. Do injured veterans deserve their government entitlements and benefits? Absolutely. Period. Injured veterans should get everything they need and more—not only from a moral obligation, but also from a contractual obligation that was in the fine print when they joined the military stating that certain benefits and entitlements are granted to them and their families. It's one of the perks of the agreement.

But that's not what I'm concerned about. I'm talking about the potentially negative identity you label yourself with if you are on this path.

Think about it. Disabled vet. What does this even mean?

Dis-abled or not-able? My friend Joe may be missing an arm, but he leads the pack in snowmobile guides in the backcountry of the Rocky Mountains. Don't tell him he's not able.

What about my friend Jason? He is a simply unstoppable Marine—and a single amputee. He deployed back into combat with a prosthetic leg, and he easily outruns his peers in the three-mile run. Don't tell him he's not able. He might be missing a leg but he doesn't tell himself he's not able.

Be careful how you label yourself because it can affect what you tell yourself about what IS and what IS NOT possible. Don't tell yourself you're not able. Maybe you have limitations but it doesn't matter. You are still capable of accomplishing great things in your life and making an impact in the world.

The truth is in the Veteran Battlefield everyone has limitations of some kind. In order to be successful, every individual has to first understand who they are and not put limits on themselves with their identity.

There are some things you will have to redefine or reinvent. But your identity needs to evolve.

Don't leave the military in the past. Take your experience into the civilian world. The Ultimate Veterans are clear on who they are and what they're about. They are clear about their accomplishments in the military and comfortable stepping up with civilians and displaying leadership.

So, what's the solution for evolving your identity? You must decide who you are. Take all your experience from the past. Nobody is exactly like you. You are a unique mash-up of all your experience. You have a lot to offer. This is your strength. Just be *you* and step up to being an Ultimate Veteran who uses those unique strengths to make an impact in the world.

Here are a few characteristics that you can identify the Ultimate Veteran by:

- Clear about who he is and what he is capable of
- Knows what he wants and goes after it
- Has a clear vision and purpose in the civilian world
- Aware of skills and strengths he learned in the military
- Knows how to apply his unique abilities to influence and lead civilians

- Defines the next level for himself
- Steps up and promotes in life after the military
- Forward thinking
- Adapts and overcomes new challenges of the civilian world
- Aware of the past but not stuck in it
- Applies military ways that are lacking in the civilian world
- Lets go of military ways that hold him back in the civilian world
- Makes an impact because he knows who he is

I'll show you later how your identity ties into your HVT.

6

Objective: Civilian World HVTs

Somewhere inside, we hear a voice. It leads us in the direction of the person we wish to become. But it is up to us whether or not we follow.
—*Corporal Pat Tillman, U.S. Army*

When SFC Tim Fagan was en route to Camp Blackhorse in Afghanistan, he didn't know for sure what to expect. He hadn't talked to anybody who had been there before that he could get the scoop from of what exactly he was getting into.

All he understood for sure was his mission. He was to teach the Afghan soldiers everything they needed to run a combat transportation company. This would include everything from teaching command structure to everything related to convoys, managing and maintaining vehicles—all the way down to the nitty-gritty basics like arranging for driving licenses, a concept that was completely foreign to the Afghans. He knew that he would be headed out on combat convoy missions with his fellow service members, kicking down doors, and moving troops from point A to point B. The danger would be high. They would often be exposed to IEDs and constantly encountering enemy gunfire.

However, Tim unexpectedly discovered the real challenge once he arrived at camp. He went on a left-seat/right-seat ride to get acquainted with the Staff Sergeant he was replacing. That's where he learned that contrary to what he had expected, the immediate threat wasn't the enemy that they would encounter on convoys but the very soldiers he was trying to train. The Staff Sergeant had received actual death threats from the Afghan commander and First Sergeant he was mentoring. Tim stepped into a role that was already hated— and with a sizable bounty placed on his head.

Tim was now an embedded trainer (ETT) and had a $70,000 bounty if he was captured or killed. Needless to say, that was a life-changing amount of money in a country racked by extreme poverty. He now understood that loyalty and betrayal and trust from the weak Afghan soldiers was a major issue.

A week later the stakes of the threat were made tragically real. Tim's chain of command Colonel and Sergeant Major were killed in a Green on Blue attack by the very same Afghan soldiers that they were embedded with. He was all too aware that he was a prime target. Within the confines of his own base, he was always watching his back and had his sidearm loaded and ready to go.

Something had to change. The people he was supposed to help were becoming the enemy. Tim amazingly had the presence of mind to take a step back from the situation and look at his orders to understand WHY he was there. Tucked into those orders was the key objective—to win the hearts and minds of the people and to train Afghan soldiers to perform their mission. He was not only there to train them to fight, but to win their hearts and minds.

Tim continued working and thinking of ways to change the climate and attitudes. One day he had a burst of inspiration. He contacted the Bishop of his church back home and came up with a plan for the members of his church. Many of them had expressed that they were praying for his safety and return. They were now able to help impact his mission in another way—by creating Operation Adopt an Afghan Soldier. The church members were thrilled to have an active role to play to support those serving their country, taking on active roles in assembling care packages. Families wrote letters thanking the Afghan soldiers for service to their country, and 130 care packages were sent from the States to the 58 Afghan soldiers that Tim was working with.

Just as the care packages were arriving, Tim went home on R&R. He brought along with him plenty of photos of the soldiers he had been serving to show to his fellow church members. They were now able to place a face with the names they had come to know. R&R came to an end and Tim returned to Camp Blackhorse. Much to his surprise he was welcomed back with smiles and embracing hugs from the Afghan soldiers. The climate had starkly changed from death threats to embracing thanks. Operation Adopt an Afghan Soldier was a resounding success and the situation was changing because Tim refocused efforts on the overall objective in Afghanistan—to win the hearts and minds of the people.

I will never forget the missions I had the privilege of serving on. I was part of an Air Assault unit and have never felt again in my life the way that I did as part of that unit. We were truly a family. A brotherhood.

Until the day a hard landing busted up my back pretty badly—and left me permanently grounded.

I felt a rush of mixed emotions on the day that I was medically retired. Part of me surely must have been relieved that I had served out my time honorably and would return home safe to my family. And yet I was frustrated that my sense of purpose had suddenly been cut short. What was I to do now?

The truth is that the transitions sucks. I was about to stick a pencil through my eye...

The truth is that the transition sucks. I was about to stick a pencil through my eye while sitting in one of the mandatory transition (ACAP) classes when I was exiting the military. The gal teaching the class listed different places to look for work related to my MOS and started talking about resume writing.

Then came the highlight when she said, "You have two options for work after you get out of the service. You can either find a job doing something similar to your MOS or you can go back to college if you want a 'real' job." Then she continued, "Civilians do a lot of the same things but they don't always call it the same, so let us help you translate your skills so you can write an effective resume."

She asked around the room for different MOS's. Many were infantry related. Some were mechanics. Others were re-fuelers and drove truck. She continued to recommend *literal* skill translations.

"Well let's see, you were in the infantry, so why don't you apply for law enforcement or security?"

"And you drove Hemmitts, so why don't you apply for driving truck or something with a CDL?"

I looked around the room and it was obvious that

there was a big lack of motivation. All the snide comments began. Not a single person was remotely excited about the future this program was suggesting.

Fast forward a few years after I bounced around among various jobs. I could always find work...*but* it was average at best and wasn't ever fulfilling. I always felt like I was just putting round pegs in round holes. I really struggled to find something more meaningful. I often reflected on the programs that help translate your military skills. I also thought about this comment: "If you want a real job, you have to go back to college." But it was also a downer to think about starting back at the bottom of the college totem pole. Sitting in class with zit-faced punks straight out of high school with no life skills just so I could earn a certificate didn't fit the experience level I knew I was already capable of.

One day I asked, "Why is that so? Why are these jobs unfulfilling and why does starting over at college blow chunks?"

Because I was capable of so much more,—and you are too.

Who will ever be fulfilled in an average job

putting round pegs in round holes after the extraordinary accomplishments they had in the military? Nobody! It won't work.

You have real skills that everyone failed to mention during ACAP and any other program transitioning out of the military.

You have mastered excellent skills like leadership, communication, planning, problem solving and so on. Most importantly, you know how to get the job done! Big jobs. Big tasks. Big missions.

They don't teach that in college. It's the real-world-street-smarts application that makes the world go around.

Don't settle for average. Because you're not. You are capable of big success in the civilian world.

Soon after I got out of the service, I moved back to my hometown where I ran into Gary—a Vietnam veteran that lived around the corner from me growing up. It had been quite some time since we had seen each other and we had fallen out of touch. After a few minutes of catching up on his life, Gary asked me "What are you doing now?"

I had been through this drill with plenty of other

people by now and I knew my lines in this scene. I whipped out my usual answer, "Well, I just retired from the military." Typically, at this point people nod their heads in admiration as if retirement is the Holy Grail of achievement. If they were civilians, they often would thank me for my service and seemed to defer to my plan of retirement. After all, in the mind of a civilian, perhaps I had earned some rest and relaxation after my service. More importantly, they left me alone and would not push the issue any further.

But not Gary. As a fellow veteran, he didn't hold my service on a pedestal above anyone else's. He wasn't playing into my game. He pinned me down.

"Good for you," he said. "But what are you doing now?"

I rambled off some different answers but he wasn't having it. I started to squirm a bit. This was uncomfortable. He continued to really pin me down and would not let his question go. I began to feel more like I was in an interrogation. When I finally ran out of my BS answers, I raised the white flag. I was speechless. I had no real answer. It was a harsh realization that I didn't have a clear objective to step up to next in life.

There was nothing next on the horizon for me at all. Not anything with real significance anyway.

At that point, I think Gary could see that I was struggling and had no real answer—not for him and not for myself. Then he said something that struck me to the core. He said, "Thanks for your service and the things you *did*. That means a lot. But it's what you do *next* that matters most!"

Gary nailed it. My military service was over and done. In the past. But my life was not over by a long shot. It was just starting a new chapter. I needed a new objective and real purpose. I needed a High Value Target (HVT) to go after next on my journey in life.

The same goes for you. Big achievements don't end for you after the military. Not for Ultra-High Achievers who mastered the necessary skills to take big targets in combat. For this rare breed of achievers, the potential for success only gets bigger and bigger in the civilian world.

The question is the same one that I sometimes have to demand of my daughters when they won't tell me what they would like to eat for dinner—what do you want?

The military gave you a gift by teaching you how to clearly define and conquer big objectives. What is your next big objective in life after the military?

It's your life. You have the freedoms of life, liberty and the pursuit of happiness. It's the freedoms for which you fought. You are free in this country to define the life you want. You choose what to do with your time and money. You get to decide what makes you happy and you are free to pursue it.

Watch out for the Objective Trap. The number one obstacle holding so many people back from progressing in the civilian world is they don't quite know what they want. The military gave them clear purpose. They knew what they wanted and had a vision of where they were going. They don't have a clear objective that they are pursuing. They get caught up in the system. They settle and go after Low Value Targets (LVTs) and long slow roads that don't lead to success. They work 50 weeks a year doing something they don't love so they can have a two-week vacation away from all the stress. They are doing what they NEED to because they just want to survive. The solution they need is to discover the next HVT to go after in life. They were capable of making an impact in the military—they saw that every day in executing the mission. Now it's time to make an impact in the civilian world. Veterans should lead the civilian world in setting clear objectives.

The key is to clearly define your next objective and new HVT. I'm not just talking about your job and your work. Whether you need employment or not, you need a purpose that allows you to continue being an Ultra-High Achiever. Otherwise you'll go nuts, much like a caged lion who is broken-spirited and loses his will. You need to continue to be challenged. You need a cause to get behind that gives you purpose and is driven by your passions and the things that excite you.

You are capable of much more in the civilian world than you think.

You are capable of much more in the civilian world than you think. You have already proven yourself in the combat battlefield. Now it's time to step up to the next level in the civilian world and make an impact. You can build any lifestyle you choose. The possibilities are essentially limitless. The question is: What do you want?

Your objective is a target, goal or outcome that you want to get to. The key is deciding where you want to go.

An objective is required before having a direction or knowing the path you must follow. Without a target, you are just wandering aimlessly. For example, when you fly somewhere on a trip, you don't start hopping random planes at the airport. You first buy a ticket selecting a specific destination.

Neither does an Olympic shooter compete by shooting in random directions—rather, they take simple but specific steps to succeed. First, they start by choosing a specific target to hit. They then use their sights to point in the right direction. Last, they commit a shot by pulling the trigger. In the Olympics, the shots are not random and every shot has a purpose. This formula leads to success.

Average Vets and Demoted Vets fail to identify

new objectives that can fully challenge themselves and make an impact in the civilian world. They settle for jobs that are not challenging even when they are fully aware that they are capable of more. They stopped growing. They don't step up and lead and make an impact. They ask what they have to do to survive instead of asking what they must do to thrive. They give up on dreams of what they really want and do what they have to do in order to just get by.

Ultimate Veterans start by pursuing their passions. They identify new HVTs that are challenging and make a difference in their own lives and to others around them. They don't just follow the paths laid out by others—they often start new organizations, new businesses, or step into executive and upper management jobs. They find ways to innovate and improve the world around them. They create vision and new missions into which they can lead other civilians. They are master problem solvers, system managers and people leaders.

There are some key problems with identifying any new objective after the military. It can be challenging to translate job skills when you exit the military. Many may take your skills only at face value without considering how they could be leveraged in other areas. For example, they might note that you were in infantry so you should apply for a job in law enforcement or security. Or if you were focused on work in transportation, why don't you try to apply for a job as a truck driver? But it's not that simple!

For example, transportation logistics in combat required much, much more organizational ability than simply driving a truck. This type of work required tactical planning, coordinating troop movements, managing enemy engagement, and much more. So simply getting out and driving a truck across South Dakota will not be as involved or challenging. It would likely be a great misuse of your talents and abilities. You would not be using many of the skills you have gained, allowing them to deteriorate.

How does it change the game if you shift your focus from a standard job to getting paid for doing what you love? Then it's not a job anymore. Who says you can't do this? Make it a goal to get paid doing something you love. It's your life. Play by your rules. Dream big.

In the military, you didn't leave your family and friends, travel halfway around the world to a combat zone, crawl through the scorching sand and get shot at simply for a paycheck. As most of us know all too well, the pay certainly isn't that good—not for all that we put on the line during our service. Rather, your objective in the military was tied to a deeply rooted cause of fighting for freedom. You fought for the freedoms of our country, our families, and our communities. Again, simply getting out and driving a truck lacks a deeply rooted cause for you to be fully engaged in. You must replace this gap by finding a worthy cause to get behind.

Your HVT Objective must have three key elements:

1.   Your HVT must be tied to your passion and interests. This is your *why*. This is the reason you get out of bed every day. If you're not passionate about it you'll never excel. However, if your HVT excites you, then your passion will be the fuel that drives you to accomplish it.

2.   Your HVT must challenge you to grow and allow you to be an Ultra-High Achiever.

3.   Your HVT must serve a higher cause and a higher purpose.

Additionally, you should also consider the following attributes for your HVT Objective:

4. Your HVT should make a positive impact on the civilian world.

5. Your HVT should be part of the legacy that you create.

You are free to design and build your ideal lifestyle. But one thing is for certain—you'll never achieve any level of success without a clear objective. You must know what you want.

What would it take to change the game from having a job putting round pegs in round holes to getting paid for what you love? Then it's not a job anymore when you get paid to do what you love. And it's a bonus when you do it on your terms.

I watched a local guy who made a career in his trophy shop selling plaques and trophies to little league teams. He didn't love it but it paid the bills. He counted down the days until retirement after which he spent full time with his lifelong passion restoring classic cars. It didn't take long until he was busier and making more money than he ever was in the trophy shop all those years. His only regret was not doing it sooner.

Dream Big. Think Big. You are used to going after big targets. Go after big targets in the civilian world! I urge you to pick a HVT that is so big it excites you and scares you at the same time. You should pick a HVT so big that you are fulfilled. You have big shoes to fill after the military.

One of my favorite sayings is, "When you love what you do you'll never work another day in your life." I try to live by it. I've seen so many people devote untold amounts of money and energy into elaborate vacation homes and excursions—to a degree that it seems clear they have constructed lives that make them so miserable they need vacations just to endure them.

So, one of my goals from early on has been to build a lifestyle from which I never needed a vacation. I am able to carry out my life's mission and make an impact on the world on a day-to-day basis while maintaining a balance of exciting adventure, hobbies and interests, and family and relationships. And I love every minute of it.

So, ask yourself these two simple questions: What is it that you want? What will you create?

7

Mission Planning: What Is Your Plan for Success?

In preparing for battle I have always found that plans are useless, but planning is indispensable.
—Dwight D. Eisenhower

March of 2013.

Lt. Col. "Dave" was the mission commander while flying an MC-12 over Zaranj, a city in southwestern Afghanistan along the Iranian border. The mission was to provide full overwatch for a Shura meeting, where two local bigwigs would get together and talk. Inside of his plane, Dave had a copilot who was steering the flight controls and a lower enlisted E-3 Sensor Operator who was also monitoring radios. Dave watched below as the first U.S. team landed at the airfield and set up security.

Then the second team landed and the U.S. VIP and escorts made their way to the vehicles and through town to the Shura at the governor's mansion.

While the Shura meeting was underway, the security team at the airfield came under fire. Unfortunately, the team at the governor's mansion was not able to communicate with their line-of-sight radios. So, Dave began to relay messages between the two teams. The multi-tasking began. Dave was doing a bit of everything—providing overwatch for the team under fire, assessing the threat, providing his fellow service members with feedback of where the enemy fire was coming from to help them be more effective, and coordinating other incoming airborne support.

Amidst all of the stress and yelling on the radios, the E-3 Sensor Operator was overloaded and he started to shut down. He could manage the sensor ball or he could talk on radios, but he could simply not do both.

Dave took over the three additional radios, and simultaneously continued to perform his duties as mission commander, monitor his copilot, support the two entities on ground, and coordinate the two air support shooters on their way.

After they accomplished their mission and all the smoke cleared, the E-3 Sensor Operator asked Dave how he was able to manage all of the radios. "Easy," Dave replied. "The names, call signs and numbers change but the format stays the same." He was proficient at radio calls that he had practiced over and over for years.

The success of this mission started in their planning and mission briefs. Not only did they plan the steps they needed to take to be successful, but Dave and his team also scrutinized every aspect of the mission and identified all crunch points where things could potentially go wrong. They spent ample time rehearsing scenarios in detail and created contingencies for each and every one of those possible weak points.

Dave completely understood from his mission planning that his young E-3 was not fully proficient. And he was prepared, knowing that he had the ability to cover the extra duties if needed to step in. The mission was a success because they had properly planned for scenarios like this.

The need for planning doesn't end after your time in the service is over. Let me ask—what is your plan for success after the military?

Here's the deal. You already know how to overtake big targets. You have proven that you can accomplish extraordinary missions in combat. You have the Ultra-High-Achiever skills necessary to win. You can execute with precision. You always adapt and overcome.

But you never did any of this without a plan. Big success doesn't happen by accident. It only happens with a carefully executed plan.

The military gave you a gift that many veterans take for granted after they get out of the service and move on to the next chapter of their lives. They taught you how to create plans to accomplish big missions and overtake big targets. They taught you how to research a situation, map out the steps, and define all the necessary details to overtake an objective. You know how to estimate requirements for people, equipment, capabilities and resources. You can evaluate risks and create plans to mitigate them. You know how to select the best action plan for success and then you back it up with PLAN B in case you need a contingency plan.

It seems like common sense, right? To you it has become second nature. It's just how you get things done. But it's not that easy for everyone else in the civilian world. You would be surprised how many people are just moving through life without a real plan. They work in jobs they don't really like. They work 50 weeks a year so they can get a two-week break and finally enjoy themselves. If this is what you want, then feel free to go for it. But you are capable of much more.

Success in the civilian world after you get out of the military is no different. The best targets in life are simply objectives that you have to map out and create a plan to accomplish.

With your abilities, you are capable of accomplishing pretty much anything in the civilian world that you want. You can create any lifestyle you want. You can run your own business or get any job you want. You can stockpile large amounts of cash. You can spend your time playing, raising your family, serving others or contributing however you want. All you have to do is clearly define your new objective and then create a plan to get there.

However, watch out for the Mission Planning Trap that most veterans fall into when they don't know how to accomplish big civilian world objectives. Sometimes they want to accomplish big things but they get the planning wrong or they give up because they don't know the proper steps. For example, many vets think in order to get upper management jobs or to start a business that they have to go back to school for graduate degrees and work their way up ladder. They try too hard to fit into what all the civilians are doing. But they lack degrees, qualifications and time in civilian service. The truth is that the steps that most civilians follow are not always the best suited for Ultra-High Achiever Vets. The civilian society indirectly puts them down and they have to start over at the bottom of the totem pole. So, what do they do? They settle.

Don't do it. Don't you dare settle for anything less than you are capable of. Your life after the military should be a promotion, not a demotion. You should step up, not be average, and not take ten steps backwards. You shouldn't struggle to just fit in and survive. You should thrive.

All you need is a good plan. A real plan. One that is detailed enough for you to execute on.

Don't overcomplicate it. It's simple. First you have to get really clear on your objective and what you want. Don't cut yourself short. You are capable of much more than you think.

Once you are clear on the objective, all you have to do is plan backwards. Map out the milestones and checkpoints along the way. Map out the requirements and resources you'll need. Define the risks and create a plan to manage them. Don't worry if you don't know the steps or don't know how to get there. Many people have already mapped the steps and walked that path before. You can learn what it takes really quickly with a little research.

When you are clear about what you want and have a clearly defined plan, then you are unstoppable.

When you are clear about what you want and have a clearly defined plan, then you are unstoppable. All that is left is to execute. Stick to the fundamentals and stay focused on the objective and you'll be a rock star in the civilian world.

With your skills you can easily be running a business or organization. You can easily get an upper management and executive job.

Our society says if you want to be successful you have to go to college. However, I say that not one size fits all. You don't always have to go back to college like most people think. The vast majority of civilians (the 86 percent that make up the workers) follow this path. For too many, they think that if they graduate college that the rest of life will easily fall into place.

That's not a plan. Consequently, the majority of people spend four years studying and racking up serious debt and after graduating can't even get a job. That is not a plan for success. It breaks my heart to see bright, young people starting out in the world already saddled by huge debt that is already placing limitations on their options and giving them stress about meeting their most basic material needs.

On the other hand, most business owners (the 14 percent of high achievers that run businesses) didn't finish college. They follow a different path and create their own businesses. They have a different perspective about the path to success. They set objectives and create plans to accomplish them. They play by their own rules.

Average Vets have a misconception about what it takes to start and run a business. They picture in their mind suits, ties, skyscrapers, boardrooms and such. They think of a corporate jerk—the boss in the movie who fires the good guy. It's the type of guy who has never gotten his fingernails dirty, who certainly doesn't know what it's like to serve under fire behind enemy lines. How could they relate to someone like that? They don't see themselves doing any of this. They think it's a whole other world in which they don't belong. They think to be successful in business they would have to go to a business college and get graduate degrees. All of this equates to the wrong idea that it takes too many years and too much work to start over and learn. This couldn't be further from the truth.

Business in its simplest form is just a matter of problem solving and creating value. And you are a master problem solver. Here are some examples. People don't have time to mow their lawns so when a kid comes along and offers to mow it, he creates value and they pay him. It's that simple. Or, people don't know how to defend themselves so they pay to learn self-defense. Or, people don't know how to fly planes so they hire people to teach them.

The path to learn how to run a successful business may be simpler than you think.

Be mindful which game you are going to play and plan accordingly. If you are going to be a doctor, lawyer or accountant, then, yes, you must go to school because the law requires it. However, there isn't a special degree to give yourself permission to start your own business. And while most of society thinks that you must get a graduate degree and work your way up the ladder for upper management positions, the truth is that most business owners really want skilled people who can get the job done and help them reach their objectives. You'll find quick success if you can problem solve and create value. You can get in quickly if you can apply your high achiever skills properly and speak the language.

If you ask any of the 86 percent what the plan to success is, they'll tell you to go to college.

If you ask any of the 14 percent the same

question, they'll tell you to go after big targets in business.

Don't worry if you don't know how. You can figure it out. You don't have to reinvent the wheel. Somebody has already figured out the path before. Find those people who are doing what you want to do and model them. Get to know them. See what and how they did it. You can copy their success and get there quicker. You just have to follow the right people. Just keep your mind open to the possibilities and give yourself permission to think big and explore your best options.

Mission planning for success in the civilian world is a cakewalk after the detailed planning you did in combat. From tactical to strategic planning, it's all about planning steps, using your resources and executing on fundamentals that will make you successful. You can be a leader in civilian world when you adapt your level of planning skills to accomplishing civilian HVTs.

I'll show you later how your planning skills tie into your HVT. For more talk on business for Ultimate Veterans see book bonuses at: www.NicTranstum.com/bookbonus

8

Capabilities: Do You Have What It Takes for Success After the Military?

There are no secrets to success. It is the result of preparation, hard work, learning from failure.
—*General Colin Powell*

May of 2002.

It was dark at 0300 when SFC Layne Morris and a couple of his guys were dug in behind a small irrigation dike in a rice field. They were just outside the outskirts of this town in rural Afghanistan, watching for the jokers who had been taking weekly potshots at their compound with RPGs.

They were alerted by two guys headed toward them about 500 yards away. One of them was carrying something over his shoulder that could possibly have been an RPG. It was a dark night and difficult to make out very much detail with their NVGs. Layne and his guys remained silently still as the enemy approached dangerously close and walked directly toward them without any clue that they were there. The tension was rising and emotions were running high as the M249 SAW gunner next to Layne slowly and quietly readied his weapon.

Layne felt the pressure of needing to make a high stakes decision. He needed to make his decision quickly. He knew that he would need to rely on his experience and wisdom to make a good judgment. He ordered his gunner to hold tight as they continued to wait patiently since they still could not positively identify the enemy weapon.

The two enemies were now so close that had they passed ten feet to either side. They would not have seen Layne or his guys. But they were headed directly toward them. Finally, at the last possible second before the supposed enemy stepped on them, Layne realized that the guy was carrying a shovel over his shoulder and did not have any weapon at all. This was, in fact, no enemy but a couple of farmers headed out to irrigate their crops. Just then, as the farmers realized they were standing over soldiers with machine guns, they reacted and started swinging the shovel to attack. Layne's SAW gunner—with his finger on the trigger and already under tense pressure—was eager to defend himself. He now had a difficult decision to make. Layne took quick action to intervene and diffuse the situation between the shovel-yielding farmer and the young SAW gunner.

In reflecting on the episode, Layne later remarked, "I'm sure glad I was out there. If I hadn't been there that farmer would have been needlessly hurt. And that kid would have to live with it the rest of his life."

"With their skills from the military, they should be upper management. Instead they are applying for low entry-level positions answering phones. They just don't know what they are capable of." I hear it time and time again from friends that run businesses.

My friend Bryan has 400 employees and is constantly on the lookout for above-average people to hire. He tells me it actually sends up a big red flag when a veteran turns in a resume and writes that he did two tours in Iraq, but he's applying for a $9 per hour job answering phones. He says, "I want to hire them. I need them leading everyone else. I need their attention to detail. I need their commitment and ability to do whatever it takes to get the job done. But if they were so capable of big accomplishments in combat then why do they undervalue their abilities in the civilian world?"

The military gave you a gift of developing many skills and abilities necessary to accomplish big missions. Here's how it worked in combat. When your boots hit the sand you knew what your objective was and what was required to take the objective. And you knew what your capabilities were to accomplish the mission. For example, you knew your team had the ability of getting to a certain location within a certain amount of time. You knew what your firepower capabilities were. You knew how long you could stay on location and when you would need reinforcements. You knew when the enemy's capabilities exceeded your own.

You don't automatically know your capabilities. You have to discover where your limits are. It's like your first day in boot camp. You start doing push-ups and running. A lot. Before long you are exhausted and muscle fatigue starts to set in. You hit the wall and can't go any further. You think you are at your limit and want to collapse, right? But then the drill sergeant yells at you and somehow you push past the pain and keep going. All day. Magically you were able to go further than you thought possible. You learned what you were really capable of. Then you trained and pushed that limit until your capacity grew. And your distance and speed improved even more.

Who gets tasked the High Value Target (HVT) missions when there is an important or risky situation? That's right...the people who are most *capable* of getting the job done. The civilian world works the same. It doesn't matter if it's a business owner looking to hire a manager, or a homeowner looking to hire a kid to mow their lawn. When anybody needs something, they are going to pay the person they think is most *capable* of getting the job done. It's that simple.

Watch out for the Capabilities Trap. If you don't apply your skills and aim at bigger targets then you'll get stuck after you get out of the service. You should be promoting in life and stepping up—not struggling to be average and just trying to fit in and survive. And certainly not applying for low-level entry jobs at the bottom of the totem pole.

You are capable of more in the civilian world than you think. As a veteran, you are an expert at getting the job done. Your skills and abilities that you mastered in the service are what the civilian world wants. They need you to get the job done. They expect you to get the job done. They believe you are capable. You need to show them you are capable.

When we first think of skills in the military we think of the obvious things like shooting targets at long range, clearing rooms, handling explosives, operating or maintaining equipment. Indeed those are excellent skills and essential to winning in combat. But what about the other skills that are often overlooked? I'm talking about leadership, mission planning, situational awareness, precision execution, focus under extreme pressure, high stakes decisions and so on.

SFC Layne Morris provided vital leadership in a situation that could have easily gone a different direction—south. A direction that could have had life-impacting consequences. But he had experience…maturity…clarity. He used good judgment.

The SAW gunner displayed his own skills. Under extraordinary stress and danger, he needed the presence of mind to be asking *himself, Do I shoot or not? Do I take action or freeze? Fortunately* he stayed calm and exercised profound discipline.

Stay aware of the Capabilities Trap. The military trained you with specialized skills and abilities to reach your objectives. You were proficient and had routine habits that get the job done. After the military, vets get stuck in the Capabilities Trap when they don't use their skills and abilities. Most often this is because they settle for a job or lifestyle that doesn't allow them to use their skills. This leads to a demotion in jobs, pay and lifestyle. The solution is to have a HVT that allows you to thrive by using your skills and excel at what you are good at. You are capable of more than most civilian jobs will give you credit for. You should lead the civilian world in capabilities.

Everyone says when you get out of the military that you should use your skills in the civilian world. The vast majority of the transition programs out there usually focus on the skills related to your MOS. This is OK. But their direction is designed to help you fit back into the LVT job market.

What everybody fails to point out are the actual high achiever skills that you developed and mastered while accomplishing missions and getting the job done. They fail to help you realize the most important skills that are required to get the job done. At the end of the day thousands and thousands of people go to school to learn. But when they graduate they run into a big problem—namely the ability to apply what they have learned in order to get the job done.

Do you realize how many employers would give their left arm for just one employee who can deliver on these qualities?

What you have in your toolbox and roster of experiences sets you apart from everybody else. You need to know that deep in your bones. You need to know that what you have is special. You have the applicable skills necessary to identify a plan and execute on major objectives. The skills you already have are the upper level equivalent of street smarts and real world application of achievement.

Specifically I'm talking about your Ultra-High Achiever skills. If you actually sat down and thought through all of the skills and abilities you offer to potential employers and customers, I will bet that you would be blown away. Think of all that you know how to do and achieve:

- You accept big responsibility
- You accept a mission or task
- You are capable of extraordinary achievement and uncommon results
- You serve a higher purpose and overall mission
- You follow values that guide how you operate and get results with excellence
- You are 100 percent committed and know what it means to never quit
- You know your limits
- You push your limits and constantly expand your capacity
- You train to create habits so results are second nature

- You learn and become proficient at whatever is necessary for mission accomplishment
- You apply what you've learned
- You are teachable and learn from constructive criticism
- You manage expensive equipment
- You manage sensitive information
- You manage people
- You are self-sufficient
- You are proficient with tactical, fundamental & strategic planning
- You can clearly define new objectives
- You can assess risks
- You take calculated risks
- You focus and concentrate under pressure
- You are situational aware and see what's going on
- You adapt and overcome
- You control your emotions
- You embrace change
- You embrace "the suck"
- You create and follow excellent systems
- You lead in teamwork, roles, and responsibilities
- You are resourceful and find solutions
- You know your core competencies and strengths
- You lead in communication

- You are confident in yourself and your abilities
- You execute with precision
- You take massive action
- You are comfortable with high stakes decision making
- You are disciplined to get results
- You execute on the fundamentals
- You have an "OCD-like" attention to detail
- You have a high tolerance to pain, fear and risk
- You are comfortable outside your comfort zone
- You are an excellent problem solver
- You get the job done
- You are a leader, role model, and visionary
- You embody moral authority and discipline
- You motivate and inspire

…and more.

These skills may seem fairly ordinary to you. You may say, "That's nothing impressive or unusual. That is just how we did things in the military. That's just how we got things done." And you would be right but in the civilian world this is not ordinary. Your capabilities are the combinations of skills, knowledge and ability to apply them to get results.

This is the stuff that makes the world go around. Do you realize how valuable somebody with all of these skills is? Do you realize how many employers would give their left arm for just one employee who can deliver on these qualities?

When you can realize how powerful your strengths are, and once you can understand your capabilities, you'll start to see new possibilities when you notice the giant lack of these in the civilian world. You'll discover opportunities all around you in the civilian world. And you can position yourself as the solution.

You'll catch yourself often saying, "People just don't get it." Or, "That would have never flown in the military." That's right. Most civilians don't get it. You are used to a higher standard of operation. But instead of complaining about it, it's your job to teach them. These are your opportunities to lead and pull them up to your level—at least in understanding.

When did you start to develop these skills? Military service is amazing in helping you to uncover talents and skills that you likely never even knew that you possessed. I remember discovering so much of what I was able to do when I was in boot camp.

I had played football and other sports in high school, but never really knew how far I could run. I had some good coaches over the years, but none of them truly pushed me to explore what I could do at my outer limits—and the stakes were never as high playing a game as they were when I was preparing to go into battle. When I entered boot camp, I quickly realized they expected me to run a lot further than I thought was possible. I never knew what the limit was though. Or in other words I never really knew what I was capable of.

How far and fast can you run? You never actually knew until one day you started running but didn't quit when you were tired or it hurt. You kept running and pushed past the pain and fatigue. When you thought you were about done and tried to stop, your platoon sergeant yelled at you to keep going. Magically you were able to push a bit further and finish. You went further and faster than you ever thought possible. You expanded your idea of what was possible. You learned your true capability. Then you trained and pushed that limit until your capacity grew. And your distance and speed improved even more.

Years down the road, after many PT tests, trainings, schools, and tours in combat, I realized that my capacity was much more than a new recruit fresh out of boot camp. What's more, even that new green soldier has much more capability than a civilian who has never been to boot camp. See where I'm going with this?

Who do you want to lead your team into combat? You want somebody with capabilities and competence that you know will get the job done. Who do you want alongside you? Who do you pick?

The civilian world is exactly the same. Who do you hire? Who do you pay to get the job done? Who do you trust? When it comes to HVTs and big objectives, you have to know your capabilities. You have to know the capabilities required to accomplish the objective. Without even knowing it, you have probably acquired these capabilities along the way somewhere. If you don't have them, then get them. Learn them yourself—hire people who have them already.

I'll show you later how your capabilities tie into your HVT.

For more details on skills and how to apply them in the civilian world check out www.NicTranstum.com/bookbonus

9

Physical and Mental Toughness: Are You Getting Weak After the Military?

I am not afraid of an army of lions led by sheep; I am afraid of an army of sheep led by a lion.
—Alexander the Great

In the early months of 2003, Colonel Randy Hansen had just arrived at Ft. Lewis when his commander walked in. He announced, "We need three surgeons in Iraq tomorrow. Are you willing to go?"

Randy only had about two minutes to make a decision that would ultimately change his life forever.

"I trained as a soldier first, for my family second, and as a surgeon third. I kept up with the physical skills required to be successful in each these duties. But just as important as the physical skills was mental toughness," he recounted. "My training had mentally prepared me and got me through the worst of the worst. The decision to deploy wasn't really a question. It was something I decided to do when I joined the military. Starting on the very first day of basic training, they prepared you for it. You know when you're up in the middle of the night doing pushups, and out running in the rain, and doing fifteen-mile ruck marches? There is some mental toughness that comes with that. It wasn't always easy. It never is. You don't want to do it, but...you just do it. It's the mental courage and willingness to do what's right."

The decision to voluntarily deploy in the face of a war that had just broken out took mental toughness. It took courage. This was entirely different business than military service during peace time, especially with a family back home to consider. But this was the whole reason he was there to begin with. And so with a moment's notice he was on a plane to Iraq.

On one particular Ba'ath Party holiday, Randy was to be transported across Baghdad. Due to the sizable security risks, nobody was to travel that day. But Randy's commander went against that advice and decided they would move anyway. "I've never feared for my life like that," said Randy. "We were all blacked out and had our weapons out the doors, as we crossed from east to west in an uncovered Humvee going about 50 MPH through the city. And I seriously thought that I was going to die. We were just sitting ducks flying across the city and my life flashed before my eyes...and I just prayed."

"I managed to get through that. And that helped me through all the four tours I did. But I'll always remember that moment that I feared for my life the most...and I knew I could do it. And I've always kept that with me," Randy remembered.

It was the same mental toughness that enabled Randy to fulfill his duties as a trauma surgeon on the front lines of the battlefield. Once again, it wasn't always easy. While there were many injured soldiers he could help, there were always those he couldn't. "You don't want to do it, but...you just do it. It's the mental courage and willingness to do what's right."

"Peace out!" I said the day I signed out of the military. No more formations. No more uniform inspections. No more 0500 PT. No more applying for travel passes to go out for the weekend. It was finally all over. I could relax. It was finally time to enjoy the freedoms for which I had fought.

Having nobody to report to can be a great thing after so many months and years in a rigid team unit. But the sudden rush of freedom can also be a bad thing. The structure that had organized all of my days was suddenly gone. I started sleeping in a bit. I ate more on the weekends because I knew there wasn't a PT test on Monday mornings. My workouts were neither as often nor as intense as they used to be. "After all," I started to rationalize, "golf is exercise, right?"

You were *tough* in the military! You had to go all around the world at a moment's notice and accomplish remarkable tasks in extraordinarily difficult situations. You were both physically and mentally tough. You had to be in peak physical condition so you could perform your duties for long periods of time without decreased performance. You were mentally tough and didn't let any danger, fear or stress distract your focus or decrease your drive. You were the well-oiled machine that you had to be to overtake such enormous challenges in combat. You had to be both physically and mentally tough in order to conquer High Value Targets (HVTs).

Frankly it's easier after all you did in the military.

You might not have thought of it this way at the time, but the military gave you a gift. They gave you a framework for physical and mental conditioning. They gave you the schedule, the steps, the challenges, the accountability and the motivation to develop peak physical and mental conditioning. They taught you how to do it and they let you practice and develop good habits. People pay good money in the civilian world for that level of coaching!

Accomplishing big success and HVTs in the civilian world works the same. Frankly it's easier after all you accomplished in the military. It's as simple as picking a target, making a plan and executing until you get it. The biggest obstacle you will have in accomplishing any success will be...*you*. You are your own biggest threat that can get in the way by limiting yourself. You should achieve a high level of success in the civilian world if you can remain a well-oiled machine.

Be aware of the Balance Trap after you get out of the service. In the military, you were physically and mentally tough. Your environment kept you balanced and focused. After the military, many vets get stuck in the Balance Trap when they become physically and mentally weak. Most often, this is due to the change in environment that lacks structure and allows poor habits and laziness to develop. You lose your framework. You lose your accountability. You lose your purpose and reason for peak conditioning. It's easy to get lazy, fat, lose focus and get lost. You become the civilian equivalent of a soup sandwich. Add the potential for PTSD symptoms to the mix and you've got a tiger by the tail. Even worse, you become less capable of accomplishing HVTs. (If you are already struggling with PTSD and need help getting your mental strength back then check out the free bonus at www.NicTranstum.com/bookbonus.

The solution is to implement a new framework into your personal life. Your environment is critical to helping you remain a well-oiled machine. You should lead your fellow citizens in the civilian world in terms of physical and mental strength. Without a proper framework, it's easy to get unbalanced in different areas of your life including your relationships with friends and family, your income and money to live, your physical and mental health staying strong, your spirituality and serving a higher purpose, and ensuring a proper balance of your time to include fun hobbies and interests.

It's easy to settle for Low Value Targets (LVTs). It's easy to quit and not stretch yourself. It's easy to find yourself not mattering like you did in the military. It's normal to find yourself struggling to fit in and survive like many veterans.

It is critical that you implement a new framework to remain a well-oiled machine.

You need a framework that will challenge and inspire you to be your best and reach your potential. You need accountability and a good coach to hold your feet to the fire when you feel like slacking or quitting. You need a good system for personal development and self-mastery so that you can continue to be a well-oiled machine and accomplish HVTs and *kick butt* in the civilian life.

I swear by a routine I follow. Your balanced core (being both physically and mentally tough) is required to pursue your HVT. You should also be interested in the framework. It deserves a separate focus elsewhere, but here is a brief outline to give you just a taste of what it's all about. There are three key areas; *Core, Domain and Impact.*

Core

Your balanced core is YOU. You must constantly challenge your physical and mental strength to remain a well-oiled machine. You need to be at your peak performance to operate at the level you want. You must constantly learn, grow and expand.

Domain

This is everything around you. Your environment

has a big influence on you and effects your lifestyle, fun, hobbies, family, and relationships.

Your life is perfectly designed to get the results it is currently getting. Good or bad, everything around you is a result of your life's system that you've created. It is important to note that you have created your environment and everything around you. Your house, your car, your couches, your pictures, your family, your friends, your bank account, your job, and everything around you is the result of actions you have taken or not taken. Like it or not, good or bad.

You should love your environment. Your life is yours to design. It's part of the freedoms for which you fought. Your environment should inspire you. You should be motivated and fueled by everything around you. If you don't like your surroundings, then fix it. You created it. You can change it.

Your domain is a world of cause and effect. It's a world of action and results. Everything great around you is the result of actions you have taken. If you have a great relationship with your spouse, love your lifestyle, and are satisfied with the amount of money in your bank account, then you have created that as well. Likewise, if you don't like your bank account, whose fault is that? If you don't like the relationship with your spouse, whose responsibility is that? If you don't like your job, whose fault is that? Everything around you is a result of the actions you have been taking. Your life is a system you've created. If you want to change any of the results then something has to change in your domain system.

You feed off of your environment. It either inspires you to step up, or it holds you back and brings you down. Either way it's your life. You can control it. You can design it. You can build it. You always have a choice.

It is your life.

Impact

This is the impact you make on the civilian world. This is your mission. This is your contribution or your business. This is the legacy that you create and will leave behind. This is the action you take and the success you make happen. Money is the result that will come from the impact you make.

What about jobs, career, and money? Doesn't everybody want me to focus on what job I will get next? What about the career I will choose next? How will I make money to live? While these seem to be important questions, it is the wrong focus.

Why do you want a job? Probably for money.

Why do you want a career? The same reason, probably for money.

Average Veterans think like this. They settle for a job they don't love, just so they can get money. They work 50 weeks a year in a job they don't love, putting round pegs in round holes, and they get two weeks off so they can take a vacation to get away from it all. Why would you want to do that? Why would you want to think like that? After the extraordinary experiences you've had and the extraordinary services you've rendered for your country, you at least owe it to yourself to consider how you can achieve an extraordinary life.

Your impact should be your focus. Why don't you build your mission around something you love? It should be something that makes a big difference for the civilian world around you, solves problems, and creates value for people. Doesn't that sound much more satisfying than a job? And guess what? If you focus on your impact, you will have plenty of money flowing to you.

Here's one of the secrets of money that everyone gets wrong. Money is not something you work for. You don't have to trade your time for money. You don't have to clock in and clock out. Money is simply a result. It is the result of the value you provide. All you have to do is focus on solving problems and creating value and you'll make plenty of money—trust me on this.

I'll show you later how your core balance ties into your HVT.

For more information, tools, framework, accountability, and community, go to:
www. NicTranstum.com/bookbonus.

10

Systems and Accountability: The Secret to Peak Performance After the Military

Every battle is won before it is fought.
Sun Tzu, The Art of War

Somebody in our battalion lost a pistol when I was at FOB Speicher in Tikrit, Iraq. They were on a maintenance test flight on a Blackhawk. They only flew traffic patterns around the airfield and never left base. After their flight had concluded, they noticed they were missing the weapon. It had surely fallen out somewhere during the flight. They knew it had to be around the base somewhere.

Was this a major issue? Absolutely. In fact, it was

so big that the war effectively came to a halt. All pending flights and missions were canceled. Everyone in our battalion was ordered to drop what they were doing at once—everyone. We were all gathered together and the search began.

We conducted what we called Hands Across Iraq. There were hundreds of soldiers. We lined up an arm's length from each other across the sandy desert and started walking. We walked the length of the runway down one side, then back up the other. Then we went to the outer berm and barbed wire that fenced off the base. We walked in the blistering heat. We set up water points and break areas for a search that stretched for days.

Eventually everyone started to ask the question, *is it worth it?* Is it worth shutting down all of our operations and dedicating so many resources to finding a single pistol that was worth only a few hundred dollars? The answer is yes. There has to be a standard somewhere. What would happen in such an operation without any accountability? What if everyone became complacent about their equipment? Or what if they lowered their standard in their duties? You can bet that such a dramatic point was made that nobody ever again considered losing a weapon or lowering their standards after that. The accountability kept everyone operating at their best.

The military gave you a gift by teaching you accountability and peak performance. Accountability is essential for peak performance and taking High Value Targets (HVT's). Big goals are tough to accomplish. Big targets are not easy to overtake. It gets discouraging. It isn't always fun and games. Sometimes you just want to quit. If big targets were easy, then everyone would accomplish them, right?

Without some form of accountability, procrastination will always set in. There are some days when you don't feel like pushing yourself. You feel like saying, *Oh, that can wait until next week*. But not if you know you'll have an inspection tomorrow. Would soldiers be in their best shape for long periods of time without mandatory PT tests? Would everyone stay proficient with their weapon without frequent qualification days at the range? Would pilots stay proficient without regular check rides?

Accountability is required to keep us operating at our best.

The civilian world works the same. Goals are

accomplished and performance is increased with the pressure of accountability. Top athletes like NFL football players and Olympic athletes all have coaches who push them to be their best and hold them accountable for their training and performance. Even business owners at the top of the food chain hire coaches to push them toward their goals. Any real level of success has some form of accountability.

It's easy when you get out of the service to spread your wings and run free. That's a good thing. No more answering to The Man, right? But who is going to push you to be your best? Who will push you to accomplish big goals in the civilian world?

Watch out for the Accountability Trap. The military provided a very structured environment for personal growth and peak performance. You were subject to constant feedback, coaching, and accountability that forced you to grow and be your best. After the military, vets get stuck in the Accountability Trap when they fail to grow and under-perform. This happens when they don't have accountability coaches that force them to be their best. The solution is to surround yourself with friends, groups and coaches who will pull you up and hold you accountable to be your best.

You should lead the civilian world in peak performance.

Without accountability it's easy to slack off, settle and not reach your potential. The problem is that you won't be happy because you know you are capable of more. You must keep achieving big targets or you will not be satisfied.

There is often a gap between what you want to do and what you actually do.

Set your sights on a big High Value Target (HVT) to go after in the civilian world. Pick a HVT so big it excites you and scares you at the same time. Then get a good accountability coach who will hold your feet to the fire and keep you performing at your best and keep you from slacking off or giving up.

There is often a gap between what you want to do and what you actually do. Accountability can help fix that.

The military was full of great examples of systems. There was a system for everything, including accountability. The systems are simply a way for everybody to get similar results. There was a system for formations. There was a system for PT. There was a system for promotions. There was a system for taking leave on weekends.

You spent many years following systems. You know good systems inside and out. You can easily create new systems in the civilian world. You can easily create new and better ways of doing things, then build systems around them. The opportunities and income generation opportunities just multiply out from there. You can teach other people how to follow the systems, then create accountability. When they are accountable they will perform and get the results you want.

You can create new routines and systems in your own life to help you maintain certain habits. And you can find people to whom you can make yourself accountable. You can find family, friends, and coaches that will encourage you to be your best.

You can create systems for putting round pegs in round holes. You can create systems that train the people. You can create systems for accountability. Then you can create systems that push the limits and discover even better ways to put round pegs in round holes. The possibilities are essentially limitless.

Peak performance, systems and accountability are highly valued in the civilian world. There is much room for improvement. You should be a leader and have many opportunities just with this simple concept.

I'll show you later how peak performance and accountability tie into your HVT.

11

Execute the Fundamentals: Money Flows Easily to Veterans Who Can Conquer Objectives

Once more into the breach,
dear friends, once more.
—William Shakespeare

In April of 2003, SGT Jeff Berntgen was driving from Iraq to Kuwait in a HETS (Heavy Equipment Transporter) convoy. The convoy had just delivered a load of M1 Abrams and M2 Bradley tanks to Baghdad for the 101st Airborne.

At one point the Lieutenant's driver stopped and approached Jeff. The driver asked, "Hey, do you know how to get us out of here?"

"Out of where?" Jeff asked.

"Back to Kuwait," the driver said. "The Lieutenant was supposed to be navigating" (managing the maps and details). "But he's been asleep for some time and I'm not sure where we are." Then he handed Jeff a stack of printer paper that somehow resembled map details.

"Can you piece us together a map and help us navigate back to Kuwait?" he asked. The Lieutenant was lost and had not even gotten out of his vehicle. They were lost because they didn't execute on fundamentals.

In the absence of leadership Jeff stepped up and executed on the fundamentals. He wasn't involved in the mission planning, but he certainly knew how a map worked. He didn't know exactly where they were but he estimated their approximate location and created a plan to move forward. And he wasn't in charge—but he *took* charge and provided leadership in the absence of it. By following simple steps they were able to piece together the situation and drive until they could confirm their location and safely make it back to Kuwait.

I didn't know if I was good enough to get into

flight school. Becoming a Blackhawk pilot in the Army wasn't automatic. It was a big goal I had but not many people get in.

I was enlisted in the Army prior to being accepted into flight school and becoming a Warrant Officer. I remember wondering if I could ever make it into flight school. I questioned if I was good enough. I didn't know if I had what it took to be selected. I had my doubts about my ability to keep up with everyone else.

Anybody who has ever applied to military flight school knows what a painstaking process it is just to apply. To say the least, it took careful planning and perseverance. Just the application process alone weeds out a lot of candidates who can't even complete it.

I'll never forget how I felt the day I got accepted. First I was shocked. Then excited. Then relieved. But I think the most pivotal breakthrough I had was realizing—truly realizing—that I was good enough. Up until this point in my life, part of me had always been waiting for someone else to give me permission and tell me I was good enough. That all finally changed with that acceptance. For the first time I gave myself permission. I decided that I was good enough and I had what it took.

My confidence and belief in myself changed that day.

Years later I can't tell you how many guys have come up to me and said, "I wanted to be a pilot…I even started an application packet once." I often ask, "Then why didn't you?"

Many of them probably had the skills to do it but for some reason didn't persevere and stick with it. I've tried to understand why they give up. Most give up with the frustrating application process. On one hand, the fairly rigorous application process is good because it weeds out people who don't rise to the task. But on the other hand, I believe most of the guys could potentially rise to the challenge if they really wanted to. But they don't. I see many of them lack confidence and don't believe enough in themselves. They fail to give themselves permission.

I have a favorite quote hanging in my office that says, *"Beginners are many but enders are few."* I keep it hanging on the wall where I can see it every time I am tempted to distract myself from a challenging project. I don't see myself as better than any of them. I just see them as beginners who failed to finish.

The military gave you a gift by teaching you to execute on fundamentals and get the job done. Getting the job done is what makes the world go around and being able to deliver puts you far ahead of many others out there in the job market.

The combat battlefield was all about execution and getting the job done. Being sloppy, weak or quitting never accomplished anything in combat. Big missions and High Value Targets (HVTs) were taken with skilled execution.

Big success and HVTs in the civilian world work the same. HVTs are accomplished with precision execution. Success comes to those who make it happen. As a veteran, you are more than capable of being successful. You have the discipline and focus that is required to *win big* if you can give yourself permission.

Watch out for the Execution Trap. The military trained you to take action and execute on fundamentals to ensure success. Skilled execution is about making success happen and getting the job done. After the military, vets get stuck in the Execution Trap when they fail to take action or fail to execute on fundamentals. Most often this is because they fail to step up to the next level, don't have clear focus, or lack discipline. Success will not come to the sloppy, weak or to quitters. Success doesn't come to the average. So don't be average. The solution is to take massive action and use your skills to accomplish your next HVT. You should lead the civilian world in precision execution.

Businesses are full of average employees who start projects. They clock in and clock out. They put round pegs in round holes. They keep busy. But they don't execute with precision.

Many people talk big. They dream big. They will always tell you how they are going to do big things. They even start. But they don't execute. They don't execute efficiently, or they don't sustain the execution and fail to finish. Then they sit around and complain about how their lives suck. That is perfectly average performance in the civilian world. It is widely accepted. But that won't cut it. You are better and capable of precision execution and getting the success you want.

Precision execution is about getting quality results. It's about efficiency and using the least amount of resources to get the job done. It's about saving time and money and still getting quality results. The civilian world is wide open with opportunity for you to bring skilled execution and get the job done! Many people will pay you lots of money to get them to those types of results.

Many steps are very simple. They are easy to overlook or get lazy and avoid. But it's the sum total of the fundamentals that leads to predictable results.

It's as simple as the fundamentals of shooting. Steady rest, sight picture, breath, control, and trigger squeeze. Follow these same fundamentals and you'll get predictable results over and over. But fail to execute all of the fundamentals and your result will suffer.

Another example of steady execution of fundamentals is easily seen in fitness. Being fit doesn't happen when you execute for a month and then quit. The gym sells one-year memberships. Their busiest month is January. The bulk of those new members aren't even there a month later—you will walk into the gym and find hardly anyone there but the dedicated gym rats who keep at it month after month, year after year. Or, you can always find good Bowflex machines at garage sales. Someone got excited about the infomercial but couldn't do the work.

The fundamentals get results but you must execute on them.

The civilian world is plugged up with people who won't get off their butts and take action.

The civilian world is plugged up with people who won't get off their butts and take action.

That can be frustrating after you have grown used to the professionalism of the military world, but it also represents a big opportunity for you. In the civilian world, money flows easily to veterans who can execute. In the civilian world, money flows easily to veterans who can execute, who can get the job done.

Getting the job *done* makes the world go around. Execution is getting the job done! Precision execution is about *how* you get the job done. Skilled execution is about quality results, less time and less money.

You are a hot commodity in the civilian world because you can execute. You get the job done. You make success happen!

People, clients and businesses will pay you lots of money to get results for them, just because you can get the job done! So don't settle for less than you are capable of. Pick your passion, strive for your dream job, or start a whole new business altogether.

I'll show you later how skilled execution ties into your HVT.

12

Resourcefulness: Where to Find the Right People and Tools to Get You There

"Greater love has no one than this—that he lay down his life for his friends."
—John 15:13

I arrived down range at FOB Speicher in Iraq in 2005, a few days after the rest of my unit got there. Unfortunately, all of the good CHU (trailers) were snatched up and I literally got stuck in a tent out back of all the trailers. This would be my home for the next year along with my roommate Kevin.

The tent was a GP Medium stretched over a wood frame with doors on the end. There was no insulation, no furniture and no air conditioning. Just a wood floor and canvas walls.

We wanted to make some improvements, but we didn't have tools or supplies. In a place without many resources, Kevin was extremely resourceful. He went around the different units until he found a saw, then a drill and some screws. He bartered for some wood somewhere and soon we were in business.

Before long, we had insulated walls and ceiling covered with sheets of plywood. We built beds for our mattresses, storage boxes, desks, a couch, and even an entertainment center with a fridge and a TV. We installed an air conditioner and ran an internet cable so we could connect to the rest of the world. By the time we were finished, it was like a nice little cabin inside. It was downright cozy, better than any of the CHUs, and many of the other guys in our unit wanted to trade with us.

They key to our success wasn't our resources. We didn't have what we needed readily available. We didn't have the tools and supplies necessary. But more importantly, we were resourceful and found the resources we needed.

The same principle applied on combat missions. We often flew in support of ground troops who needed reinforcements, more bullets, air support, and more firepower. There were often situations where our guys didn't have enough resources immediately with them. But with good communication, radios, helicopters, and resourcefulness, we were always able to find more supplies or more teams necessary to complete the mission. That's how you win and accomplish your objective.

The military gave you a gift of being resourceful. They taught you to be connected and engaged with your team. Not only did you need them but they needed you.

Everyone knew their role and their place in the team structure. In combat there are those who lead it. Those who plan it. Those who execute it. Those who protect it. Those who feed it. Those who transport it. Those who communicate it. Those who focus on and shoot it.

You can't do all the research. You can't know all the various skills. You can't do all the execution.

You can't do it all yourself. You need a team.

The pursuit of your HVT is the same. You don't have to do everything yourself. You can't. You need people and resources.

Watch out for the Resource Trap. The military trained you to be connected and engaged with the people and resources necessary to carry out your mission. You either did the job yourself or you found the right person who could get it done. After the military, vets get stuck in the Resource Trap when they aren't connected to the right people or resources. Most often this is because they have limited civilian world resources and they give up. The solution is to find and connect with the best civilian world people and resources necessary to carry out your new HVT mission. The key is to do whatever it takes to find the solution you need. You were resourceful in the military and you need to be similarly resourceful in the civilian world to be effective. You should lead the civilian world in resourcefulness.

Just like HVTs in the military, you won't be able pursue your new HVT by yourself. You need to surround yourself with people who will help you get there and accomplish the big missions. These people will become your new team. They can be veterans or civilians. All that truly matters is selecting the people that have the skills you need to help you accomplish your new missions.

It's time for you to create your own vision and

define your own mission. It's time for you to build your own team to carry out the mission and get you there.

You don't have to know everything. You just need to know what the mission is and take charge of getting there. You are the new commander.

You don't have to know everything. You just need to know what the mission is and take charge of getting there. You are the new commander. You hold the vision and steer the ship. You can hire people with the right skills to help get the work done.

You have many options. You can hire your own employees or you can hire other businesses to do certain things for you. You can hire short-term or long-term. Whatever you need, you can buy it.

You don't have to be good at everything. With the right people in the right positions, they will have more fun doing what they love and they're probably better at it anyway. Lead them. Tell them what you need. Then get out of their way and let them do their job.

For now, you just need to realize that being resourceful will help you accomplish your HVT.

13

The Art of Identifying Your Next HVT

"…it's not enough to fight for a better world; we also have to live lives worth fighting for."
—*Governor Eric Greitens, former Navy Seal*

We have discussed nine gifts that the military gave you that are your key to pursuing your next HVT. These are critical steps you have to take. If you don't use all of them then they become traps that hold you back.

The art is your spin. Your rules. Your definition. Your Game.

It is quite possibly a difficult task since everyone else has always identified what the objectives were for you. You've answered to *the man* long enough. Now it's time that you be *the man* and define your own objective.

These are all the elements that make up your HVT. Now we are going to bring it all together and talk about the art of identifying your HVT to move your life into high gear and show you the keys to rapid success in the civilian world.

The art of the whole process is making it yours. It's your identity. It's your objective. It's your passions. It's your ideas. It's your plan. It's your HVT.

1. Challenged – Define a HVT that fuels your passion, pushes your limits, and allows you to grow and expand. You are an Ultra-High Achiever. You must be challenged. You know you are capable of more. You will not be satisfied with mediocre nine-to-five jobs putting round pegs in round holes. You should lead the civilian world in high achievement.

2. Identity – You will excel in the civilian world when you are clear on who you are and what you are about. You should lead the civilian world with your clarity and confidence in your identity and knowing who you are and what you are about.

3.   Objective – Identify what you want to go after next in life. You were capable of making an impact in the military so now it's time to make an impact in the civilian world. You should lead the civilian world in setting clear objectives.

4.   Plan – Create a plan to go after your HVT. Don't get stuck if you don't know the way. Find somebody who has already accomplished what you want and model them. You should lead the civilian world in effective mission planning.

5.   Capabilities – Thrive by using your skills and strengths to excel at what you are good at. You are capable of more than most civilian jobs will give you credit for. You should lead the civilian world in capabilities.

6.   Balanced – Implement a new framework into your personal life. Your environment is critical to helping you remain a well-oiled machine. You should lead the civilian world in physical and mental strength.

7.   Peak Performance – Surround yourself with friends, groups and coaches who will pull you up and hold you accountable to be

your best. You should lead the civilian world in peak performance.

8. Execution – Take massive action and execute on fundamentals. Use your skills to accomplish your next HVT. You should lead the civilian world in precision execution.

9. Resourcefulness – Connect with the best civilian world people and resources necessary to carry out your new HVT mission. You were resourceful in the military and you need to be resourceful in the civilian world to be effective. You should lead the civilian world in resourcefulness.

I can guarantee you that if you are stuck, not satisfied, wanting more, or even struggling in the civilian world after the military it is because one or more of these gifts is going unused.

Go through each of these nine steps and define it. It may take time. Get clear. Get real. Decide what you want. It's your life, liberty and pursuit of happiness. It's the freedoms for which you fought.

When you use each of these nine gifts, you harness the power to step to the front of the line.

Here are some ideas to get you started today.

Take your passion and build a business related to your HVT. The skills that you have learned over the course of your service will allow you to hit the ground running in the business world.

- Take your business online and nationwide.
- Open a franchise of an existing business that you love.
- Create your own training program.
- Start your own tribe of fanatics that have the same interests.
- Coach and mentor people in your passion.
- Get a HVT job—one that aligns with your greatest skills and goals—and join a team that is already pursuing your same interests.
- Apply for upper management positions where you can be a leader and help inspire others to fulfill their greatest potential.
- Join a non-profit and get on their board to help provide leadership to their mission.
- Start a non-profit and create a new meaningful cause.
- Engage local and community organizations and find ways to help them

improve.

What's your passion? What's something you love to do that you would do every day if you could get paid for it? What's something about which everyone always your advice? What's something you love to learn about? What's something that's easy for you but not easy for other people? What experiences do you have that other people don't that you can teach them about? What challenges have you overcome that you can help other people grow through?

What does success mean? You define that. *Never* let anyone else dictate if you are successful or not. You don't have to make a million dollars if you don't want to. But be honest with yourself. If you want to make it—then you should. There's nothing holding you back from reaching your fullest potential other than yourself. But you should do it because YOU want to and not because anyone else tells you that's what you have to do to be successful.

You're already successful in measures beyond most anything found in the civilian world. You already proved yourself in combat and delivered under the toughest conditions known to man. All you need to focus on is where you are today and where you want to be tomorrow. And improve yourself one day the time. And enjoy the ride. If you can accept that you're already successful and be happy with who you are right now, then the pursuit of your next HVT will be a lot more fun.

You buy the house you want. You drive the cars you want. You wear the clothes you want. Be you. In fact the more secure you are with your identity, the more people will be drawn to you. But that attraction goes away as soon as you start doing things that don't represent you just to please other people. If you want to wear a suit and tie, then great! But if it's not you, then rethink your plan.

Maybe you need to expand your vision of what's possible. You have already proven you are capable of accomplishing big missions. This is just a matter of selecting a new big mission. Don't limit yourself. You are capable of accomplishing more than you think.

What are you passionate about? You have to contribute. Matter. Lead. Make a difference. Influence and impact.

You can have all the money you want. But learn this lesson. Listen carefully—do not chase money. There is a money trap—simply running faster on the wheels to keep up with a hunger that you can't ever fully satisfy. Focus on creating value and money will follow. Create more value and you'll get more money. Money is a result of the value you create.

Pick a mission so big it excites you and scares you at the same time. Make it something that energizes you to spring out of bed each morning. Dream big again like you did when you were a kid.

Why not? You are in America, after all—the land of the free, full of wide-open fields and endless possibilities. With your capabilities, you are limited only by your own vision and what you see as being possible for yourself.

Don't worry if you don't have it all planned out. You don't have to know all the answers. Just pick something and get after it. Move forward. It's okay if you change your objective months or years down the road. Just don't get stuck doing nothing. One path may lead to another. You may find something bigger and better to go after. You will continue to evolve.

Always remember the many benefits of a good

HVT. You will have purpose. Drive. Opportunity. Community and camaraderie. You will be valued and matter. Leave a legacy. Make your mark. Excite others. Provide vision. Lead. Inspire.

What if your military experience only prepared you for what lies ahead?

14

Final Thoughts

Old soldiers never die; they just fade away.
—General Douglas MacArthur

When I see Demoted Veterans begging on street corners with their disabled vet signs, I always wonder to myself, *What happened? How did you get here?*

My heart aches. I so want to help them. But I know giving them five bucks isn't going to fix their problems.

Part of me wants to grab them by the shoulders and shake them while screaming, "Wake up, my brother! You are part of a rare breed! You are a true warrior that proved yourself in combat. You have what it takes to conquer big challenges. You just have to believe in yourself and see the path forward."

And when I see Average Veterans struggling to fit in, not stepping up, not conquering like they did in the military, I have to ask, *What happened? You are part of a rare breed. You are capable of so much more. You have what it takes to conquer big challenges. The civilian world needs you to step up and lead. You just have to believe in yourself and see the path forward.*

God bless our brothers and sisters who struggle. I know what that feels like. I wish someone would have given me this book when I transitioned. It would have saved me literally years of struggle.

Luckily you are different. Now you know better. I have shown you the way. You have a choice. And to you I say...

You are part of a rare breed. You are a true warrior. You have proven yourself in combat. You just have to believe in yourself. You know the path forward. Step up to your next HVT in life.

The civilian world badly needs your leadership. You are a powerful force for good. You have what it takes.

You are the Ultimate Veteran.

You are not alone. Without a discovery of who you are and your next step and purpose then you will flounder, get lost and bounce around in society. You will doubt. You will ask, *Did I matter?*

When you are clear about who you are and you know your purpose, then you are unstoppable.

The Ultimate Veteran understands and lives the three rules of a veteran. He understands that his or her work is not over, but just transitioning to the next chapter. The mission for freedom continues and he answers the call and steps up. He honors his own sacrifice and the sacrifice of his brothers by understanding and living the freedoms for which they fought and stepping into the next mission.

The truth is that you mattered then—and you still matter now. Your country still needs you. Now, more than ever.

The day-to-day grind is a world of people just trying to win at life the best they know how. They understand their freedoms but they are often trapped in their own rat race just trying to keep up. They have kids. They have to please the boss, pay the bills, buy formula and diapers—all while placing their most cherished dreams and achievements on the back burners.

They get an occasional fun time, an escape away from the routine, maybe in a sunny locale. But they are still locked into a perpetual cycle of grind to survive. They get stuck.

They are in dire need of a reminder of their freedoms. They need role models. They need super heroes. They need leadership.

They need to believe in their freedoms, create their own dreams again. They pursue what they believe will make them happy. With all the noise and confusion of moral rights and wrongs, and confusion of what freedom is, our county is in critical need of leaders who believe through and through what it's all about and how it really works.

It needs veterans and patriots who still love the flag, who are willing to go around the world and put their lives on the line to protect it.

But it doesn't end there.

It needs those same patriots to take their knowledge of freedom and stand as a beacon and lighthouse. They alone among our citizens have the moral stature that comes with putting their lives on the line for freedom.

Veterans must take our citizens by the hand, rise above the drama, and teach the American people what is necessary to build the American life.

Such leadership is not easy. It will surely be criticized as it challenges the corrupt agendas and ideals of many radical and alternative lifestyles today. It requires a strong force of individuals who are battle hardened, clear purpose driven, disciplined in values and processes, willing to stand on the wall and say, "You won't destroy my country. Not on my watch."

Freedom requires true leadership—not by force and pushing, but by standing solid and leading by example. It requires someone who is not afraid to stand. Not afraid to be criticized for their beliefs. Willing to protect. Who better than those who have mastered these skills and learned the meaning of these principles on true battlefields? Who is better qualified to lead than the veterans who are willing to step up to the next level? Who better than those who are clear on their next mission? Who better than the Ultimate Veteran?

So thank you for your service. And thank you for your service that is still to come.

Go live the freedoms for which you fought.

Identify your next HVT to pursue.

And make an impact in the world.

You are the Ultimate Veteran.

Thank you for going on this journey with me.

Nic

WHAT'S NEXT?

Share this book with a friend.

Get your free book bonuses, videos and training
at www.NicTranstum.com/bookbonus

For information about purchasing this book in
bulk, educational materials, training or speaking
contact us at www.NicTranstrum.com

 NIC TRANSTRUM

ABOUT THE AUTHOR

Nic Transtrum was a Blackhawk pilot in the US Army. He served in Iraq with the 101st Airborne Division.

He built his first *6-figure* online business from his tent in Iraq during downtime between missions.

His most recent accomplishments include creating UltimateVeteran.com and helping other veterans step up and live the freedoms they fought for.

He lives in Idaho with his wife and six daughters.

 NIC TRANSTRUM

Made in the USA
Middletown, DE
13 March 2018